THE HILL

CW00890752

ff

TOM PAULIN

The Hillsborough Script

A Dramatic Satire

faber and faber
LONDON · BOSTON

First published in 1987
by Faber and Faber Limited
3 Queen Square London WC1N 3AU

Photoset by Wilmaset Birkenhead Wirral
Printed in Great Britain by
Cox and Wyman
All rights reserved

British Library Cataloguing in Publication Data

Paulin, Tom
The Hillsborough script.
I. Title
822'.914   PR6066.A884
ISBN 0–571–14943–X

I could start with a star-shaped artillery fort, a green hill, a soldier called Moses. Knighthood, sword, knapsack and flag. A document awarding him several thousand acres of confiscated land. Helmeted and experimental, he moves through long grass, a metal appetite, a male machine that mows. The grass parts before his eyes like breasts.

The heirs of Sir Moses Hill set up a garrison or 'architecturally elegant small town, 6 km S. of Lisburn, with a spacious wooded park (with trout) and an eighteenth-century house that accommodates members of the Royal Family and visiting foreign diplomats'.

Itemized on the inventory are:
sentry boxes
wrought-iron gates
scanners
foodshops
church
filling station
some Reynolds cherubs
two newsagents
naked baby by Nollekens
market house
The Downshire Arms
dry cleaners

They add into a small town with a watchful, too clean, tight and precious air to it. Union bunting stretches across the main street, the raised portraits of Queen and Duke give them Ulster faces and stooped uncertain shoulders, but the feel of the place is strangely English, its spirit strained and confused, an outpost of the capital. And the name feels wrong, a social flourish or italic signature over the gilt Jacob's ladder on the triumphal arch.

One winter, a rushed evening four or five years back, I find myself in London. It's dark, heavy, hurried, smelling of money and appetite. I'm sucked into a building somewhere off the Strand. It feels like a club – marble, gold leaf, big flowery mirrors, a staircase to an arched room where a politician – a spent Ulster one – grins as he launches a fantasy product in paperback. Wine and buzz, lots of buzz. An ugly tub of slime has written an ugly book. Might be worth dipping into. Call him the Budgie. Some kinda supergrass.

I listen to him swapping man-jokes with one of our local press barons. The baron turns to me and asks, 'Are yu an Ulsterman?' I can say neither yes nor no and slip away. Another politician – not spent, running the province, a familiar pouchy face simulating *gravitas* in public – is drunk and fed up. He coos, he talks, he sings. A cushat voice faked from out one of the minor changing-rooms of an ageing civilization – a lounging, confident, really rather sweet and mellow rendition of somebody else. I admire ye, master of the tides.

Awful dump, he confides, can you imagine? . . . meeting the likes of Paisley and Molyneaux day after bloody day. Ack it must be desperate. And the duty weekends – they're the real thing bad. Stuck in the drawing-room at Hillsborough of a Saturday night . . . *Brideshead* on the video, eating a ghastly Ulster fry in the company of several equally ghastly *Ulster* civil servants. Quite immoral they find it. Jack Hooper, Bill Hooper, Sam the Grass . . . I've given them all nicknames. They don't like it, not a bit. Why, only the other day one of them stood up and said, *It's disgustin' this – I'm goin'.* Dear little chap toddled out and left me alone with an extremely large bottle of Black Bush.

So whose side are you on? The bored politico left with bottle and image of Christchurch Meadow, or Disgusted, the native – is that the right word? – civil servant who walked out of the drawing-room? A man no doubt typical of his class, that servile, demoralized, parasitic crowd, the Unionist middle class. A people clinging to a vanishing Britain – white, imperial, brisk, Anglo-Saxon. How they hate art and ideas, those wee provincial philistines in their Orange Free State. Didn't that rasping little man walk out because he couldn't take having his nose rubbed in all those *Catholic* images any longer? Imagine siding with him. Imagine *not* siding with the tidal master, far from home, trying to relieve the dreadful tedium of the six counties.

The figure who spoke of that tedium was all gaps and flashes, his smoked vowels discontinuous with wherever or whoever the rest of him might be. Without maybe knowing it, he embodied a deep and current scepticism about the integrity of human character. Personal identity makes no sense at all, especially to the bundle of accidents shuttling between two islands. We speak, or we're spoken, in bits and pieces, and nothing adds up. But the minion who walked out, the disgusted civil servant, he saw himself down his own tunnel vision as a definite shape formed by a belief – a belief that was not being ratified by his superior. His narrow private corridor was lit by his illusion of being an honest soul. His superior, though, pretended to believe, and then only in what he happened to be uttering in the moment, like an actor in a trapped game being played out during a country-house weekend. But the other one became himself by walking out on the game. He freed himself by making an act of choice.

It's known that Stafford Cripps had to stick a coal scuttle on his head when the entire Labour cabinet was bid play charades one weekend at Balmoral . . . he had to endure that particular humiliation at the word of the now Queen Mother. But the refusal of the civil servant to sit out the rest of his nose-rubbing evening – I sympathize with that. It's what made me start writing, in the summer of 1985.

A few months later – on 15 November – the Anglo-Irish Agreement was signed and the little town of Hillsborough was famous for five minutes. This series of displaced dialogues is an attempt to swim out among the sounds and surfaces of a political moment on a green hill that is south of Belfast, north of Dublin, and very far away from the other capital.

CHARACTERS

BIMBO	Secretary of State for Northern Ireland
INDIA	his assistant
HERBY	the gardener
NORMAN	an Ulster civil servant
AUSTIN	the Gook or GOC
CHIEF CONSTABLE	Copperbottom
KEN HENDERSON	a member of the Eastern Health and Social Services Board
BERNI	a photographer, played by actress who plays India

ACT ONE

An upstairs drawing-room in a country house which used to be
occupied by the Governor of Northern Ireland. It is early July,
mid-afternoon. White carpet, red, white and gold striped
wallpaper which contrasts with the Draylon tackiness of the
pink curtains that hang down beside the three windows on the
back wall. On the wall between the windows, left, hangs a
portrait of the Queen, and on the wall between the windows,
right, there is a large map of Northern Ireland. Under the map
there is a teleprinter which spits out long print-outs at times (a
buzzer sounds when news is particularly urgent). The windows
open out on to a yellow sandstone balcony filled with plants,
creepers, bay trees in earthenware pots. The centre of the room
is dominated by a large *chaise-longue* in front of which is a low
coffee table. On the table are a silver cigarette box, an ashtray,
cigarette lighter, a white plastic unfinished model of a jumbo jet,
and a saucer containing water and decals. Underneath the table
is a pile of today's newspapers. Against the wall, right, there is a
mahogany desk on which are several differently coloured
phones, papers, two red dispatch boxes, an orchid, a small
computer screen and keyboard, cups of pens and pencils, a
plastic ruler, a grey machine for sharpening pencils, a box of
chocolates and a small round mirror on a tubular stem. A
handbag and two glossy black carrier-bags stuffed with
tissue-wrapped objects are stowed casually against the wastebin
beside the desk. Between the desk and the door there is an ochre
filing cabinet. Left there is a small cubby-hole pantry from
which drinks and snacks are obtained. There is a bathroom
beyond the pantry. Against the wall, near the pantry door,
stands a delicate walnut escritoire on top of which is a grey
cactus. A tall Kentia palm arches from the escritoire towards the
chaise-longue. A few table lamps and/or standard lamps, an
eighteenth-century Watteauish oil painting on one wall.
  Enter HERBY, a gardener in washed-out blue overalls,
carrying a watering-can. He is a big man in his fifties with black

hair and a face weathered by air, sun, hooch. He has a mischievous, lidded smile and large, cute hands. Though he is obviously familiar with the room and at ease in it, he moves with the neat, tight vigilance of a cat burglar. Setting the watering-can by the palm as a pretext for his presence, he takes a cigarette from the box and lights it with the lighter while glancing at the teleprinter. Replacing lighter on coffee table, he crosses to the desk and glances through some of the papers on it. Then he opens the middle drawer of the filing cabinet, riffles through the files, takes one sheet out, reads it carefully, then puts it back and closes the drawer. Next he presses the computer keyboard, reads the screen and cancels the image as he picks up the white phone. He taps a number while flicking through the papers on the desk.

HERBY: (*Squinting at sheet of paper*) Hey, Ernie?

It is, aye. How's the form?

Oh, grand.

Where'm I ringin from? – sure y'know, Ernie . . . thon new payphone in the stables – nah, y'stick a card in just. (*Rubs finger on dispatch box.*) Hey, look, I'm chasin' some bullwire – have y'any in stock, have yu?

(*As he talks and listens,* HERBY *moves about the room carrying the phone casually in one hand and flicking the flex deftly like a lariat.*)

Aye, chainlink, that's right.

Nah, nah – these gardens? Nah, it's for myself, like. I'm buyin' some yos.

Jesus, I'll set a ram on them.

One? – aye – sure . . . could dart upta fifty in the one day. Offa this fella owns the big fillin' station near us . . .

Aye, that's right, Jim Samson . . . aye.

'Bout seven acres I'm gonna rent off him.

Nah, it's just t'separate one field uppa bit – could y'give us sixty-five yards, say? (*Moving back to desk*)

Aye, metres.

How many's that? (*Taps keyboard quietly.*) Sixty?

(*Freezes.*) Hold on! (*Taps keyboard.*) OK, sorry – someone was callin' me.

2

Nah, don't want the plastic. Give us the galvanized.

What gauge! Jesus, Ernie, you tell me! Anyone'd think it was a fuckin' railway I'm orderin' – steada justa bitta ould bullwire – sorry, chain*link*.

Aye, plus vat.

Ack, that's very gooda you, Ernie. So it's just (*Tapping keyboard*) 65 times 2.12? how much is that now?

127 pound, 20 pence. Grand. Dead on. Yep. Right y'are.

That'd be great, Ernie – say, Tuesday. Just leave it backa the house if she's not in.

Thanks very much now, Ernie.

See you, Ernie. Thanks Ernie.

(*Replaces phone, moves closer to door, listens while stroking door with one finger, then moves back to phone, lifts it and taps number.*)

That Texel?

(*Hard, suspicious*) Texel what?

(*Appeased*) Aye, Swatragh . . .'s a fly man. (*Looking at papers again*) I've not got much for you the day.

Portiedown! Sure it'll be no different this season – fact he's fillin' the new guy in this evenin'.

Aye, (*Moving centre of room with phone*) that's right, aye.

New GOC, that's right, aye. Know what he calls him?

Crum the fuckin' tenth! Don't be stupid! The Gook, that's what he calls him. The Gook. Aye.

Jesus, how would I know? I'll find out but –

– in a coupla hours just. (*Pauses.*) Here, hold on – I can hear something.

(*Places phone and receiver lightly on carpet and slowly removes cigarette from the silver box, pats breast pockets automatically for matches, can't find them, uses lighter on coffee table.*) Sorry, thought there was someone in the main office.

Nah, hard t'say.

Oh he's up t'something OK. Can't figure it out but. He's been spendin' a lotta time in the green room lately – aye, fer hours, talkin' wi'Dublin.

Aye, that's right, sure. Yeah, a lotta time.

I reckon he wants use the Gook t'put one over on him . . .

3

Aye, on the Chief Constable, that's right.

Something t'do wi'money and Capitol Hill and that fella wi' those American baked beans. There's this scrappa paper (*Reaching into breast pocket*) . . . I found it yesterday in th'wastebin . . .

What's it say? (*Unfolding it*) Oho now – (*Squinting*) sure his writin's worse'n mine. (*Holds it up to light.*) 'Blood and . . . pleasure?' . . . nah. Leisure? – nah, doesn't look right. Treasure – aye, treasure. 'Blood and Treasure'. That's it. Others're only scribbles – 'cept the bottom one says 'Termi . . . Terminal Impatience'. Any use that?

Aye, we can all guess. It's great crack guessin'.

See what I can hoke out! Jesus this is more'n he usually leaves behind him . . . they put nothun on paper those boys.

Phone ye! I won't get another chance! Not today. Jesus, the risks I'm takin' – for Ulster!

OK, OK . . . OK. Henderson. Right.

After the reception. Right. You tell your Mr Henderson.

Nah, have to be outside . . . in the gardens. Down by the lake . . . there's this big chestnut. Tell Henderson. He can wait on me there.

Right. Sure he can pretend he got canned and then wandered off.

OK. Right. I'd better head.

Right. See you.

(*Puts phone down, moves left and picks up watering-can, starts to pour, stops almost immediately as if he's heard something, pours again, then exits nimbly to balcony just as sounds of conversation gather off-stage right. Enter* BIMBO, *a heavy post-prandial waddle. Followed by* INDIA *who carries a leather portfolio.* BIMBO *is a large man with tousled hair, a glistening lower lip and a confident, sometimes squeally, Oxford voice. He wears a floppy bow-tie and a double-breasted suit.* BIMBO *is in his late forties and has been Secretary of State for more years than he cares to remember.* INDIA *is about twenty-nine years old, very thin, with short blonde hair and tight metal earrings. She wears a black pencil skirt and a white T-shirt. Her voice is*

4

an uneasy compromise between girls' public school and London suburban, and her manner often has a brittle platinum sheen.)

BIMBO: Mineral, yes. With ice. (*Goes to teleprinter, scans print-out casually.*)

INDIA: (*Looking at papers in portfolio, sitting down on rotating chair at desk*) Eh? what d'you say?

BIMBO: (*Scanning print-out*) Ice.

INDIA: Yes, ice. So?

BIMBO: (*Looking up*) Sweetie, I'm asking you to fix me a glass of Perrier . . . with ice . . . (*Looking at print-out*) . . . with leemon.

INDIA: (*Concentrating*) Mintin, mintin.

BIMBO: (*Flicking print-out back*) God, the bloody bumf they wire through! Anyone'd think I'm some sort of rally driver! . . . do I really need to know that Rolls-Royce have discovered a way of seeing inside a running engine? (*Moves to chaise-longue and subsides.*)

INDIA: You don't . . . (*Getting up, concentrating on sheet of paper in her hand, moving towards pantry*) . . . you most certainly do not. (*Exit.*)

BIMBO: (*Scrabbling in box for cigarettes*) Transparent engines . . . X-rays . . . one simply wishes not to know.

INDIA: (*Entering with glass of Perrier*) Voilà!

BIMBO: (*Mimics*) Ack, thank you, now. I'm awful grateful. (INDIA *sits down and begins to pluck her eyebrows,* BIMBO *shakes his shoes off, lights cigarette and lies back again.*) Who's on the menu? – anyone?

INDIA: Mmm – enough. (*Drops tweezers accidentally.*) Oh bugger! – that was your fault, Bimbo. Why can't you stay with the silence for a tiny while? (*Handing a piece of paper*) Here – catch.

BIMBO: (*Taking hold easily and not reading*) I just loved the way you dropped that artichoke – (*Moving hand smartly downwards*) – right in the Lord Mayor's crotch.

INDIA: (*To mirror*) Probably thought I was making a pass . . . God, what a creature!

BIMBO: Nice artichokes, though. Always like them with a touch of oil. (*Reading*) Oh God! – the Gook. *And* old Copperbottom.

INDIA: Artichokes *farci* – much superior.

BIMBO: (*Sighing*) Too rich, too rich. Mind you, (*Casting paper towards table*) ghastly though he was your little Lord Mayor did have one very interesting idea –

INDIA: (*Sceptical*) Did he really?

BIMBO: Mm. We'll be out of here even sooner than I thought.

INDIA: I don't believe you.

BIMBO: Ask his lordship – he wants to twin Belfast with Dublin.

INDIA: He doesn't!

BIMBO: Oh yes he does. I rather warmed to the little fellow. Started talking about the twin-town, twin-city idea . . . I said, yes, seems to have caught on terribly well back home. One goes up into the Chilterns and comes across all sorts of tiny tiny villages twinned with places in France or Germany. 'Oh I agree – isn't it a great idea? – Belfast wi' Dublin – I ask ye!'

INDIA: But isn't he one of those dreadful loyalists?

BIMBO: Yes, but he's absolutely set on the idea . . . so (*Motioning to row of phones*) give Dublin a buzz, there's a dear.

INDIA: Don't you think we'd better check it out first?

BIMBO: No, no – just get me the Taoiseach.

INDIA: I do think we ought to sound out that little Permanent Secretary chappie.

BIMBO: (*Sagging*) Oh Norman! Do I have to?

INDIA: He *is* writing a speech for you.

BIMBO: Have to see him anyway, I suppose. Oh, give him a buzz, do.

INDIA: (*Pressing buzzer*) Could you send Norman up – pronto – please?

BIMBO: (*Puzzled*) Come to think of it some of what the Lord Mayor said didn't quite make sense – but who does over here? Started muttering about fuzzy wuzzies – lots and lots of fuzzy wuzzies –

(*Knock at door, enter* NORMAN, *an anxious Permanent Secretary in a tweed suit. He exchanges a formal, embarrassed nod with* INDIA.)

6

(*Rising slightly*) Norman! my dear fellow – do take a pew.

NORMAN: (*Sitting down nervously on one of the new armchairs and speaking with a soft steely politeness*) Thank you, Secretary of State.

BIMBO: (*Fierce*) Like 'em, do you?

NORMAN: (*Muttering*) Yes, I must say . . .

BIMBO: (*Not listening*) I was opening some dreadful reception in one of your larger department stores last week when I bumped into them. Beautiful polished leather, don't you think? And the chrome frame? – quite superb. Oh yes, we grow our own timber here. We frame our own frames. Quite the chrome de la chrome up here we are. And d'you know what they say, Norm?

NORMAN: (*Uncertain*) Oh, I'm not . . .

BIMBO: (*Pouncing*) 'When in Chrome do as the Chromans do.' That's my maxim. Based my entire policy on it so far.

NORMAN: (*Mild demur*) I don't think . . .

BIMBO: Norman! I've warned you before – you don't think. I will never never never allow a mere civil servant – and an *Ulster* one at that – to believe for one second that he has a mind of his own. D'you hear me?

NORMAN: Could I just say, Secretary of State?

BIMBO: (*Annoyed*) No, you fucking well can't say. Listen – Bimbo is Bimbo. (*Sits up, scratches armpits.*) Bimbo thinks, Bimbo does, Bimbo disposes, Bimbo smells. Bimbo mixes with bloody Rotarians . . . Bimbo asks Norman to write memos in his best Rotarian prose. And what's more (*Pauses.*) . . . Oh God (*To* INDIA) give the poor bugger a glass of retsina. (*Flops back.*) I'm absolutely exhausted.

INDIA: (*Handing* NORMAN *a glass, pouring wine into Bimbo's glass*) Really we just wanted to check an idea with you – we're about to announce that the city of Belfast is going to be twinned with the city of Dublin – what d'you say?

NORMAN: (*In a level official voice*) I think it might inflame an already tense situation.

BIMBO: (*Sitting up and smiling smugly*) You're out of touch, Norm. Way out. The Lord Mayor of Belfast put it to me this very lunchtime –

7

NORMAN: He wanted to twin with *Dublin*?

BIMBO: Dublin, yes. That's what I said.

NORMAN: You mean that's what you heard.

INDIA: (*Looking at Bimbo*) Oh no –

BIMBO: Oh God! it's that awful accent again . . .

INDIA: It wasn't Dublin!

NORMAN: (*Smiling*) It was Durban. South Africa – he loves the place.

BIMBO: (*Slumping*) Hence the fuzzy wuzzies. Of course. And the 'Homeland and the homelands'.

INDIA: God, they're so abrasive, aren't they, those little men? Most of them have hair like steel wool anyway. Hard but fuzzy. Talking to them's just like chewing on a Brillo pad.

NORMAN: (*Rising*) If you'll excuse me –

BIMBO: (*Clicking fingers*) Norm, I want you back in ten minutes – bring that wretched speech with you, d'you hear?

NORMAN: It's almost complete, Secretary of State.

BIMBO: Good–good.

(*Exit* NORMAN.)

So fuzzy *and* emotional, these Ulstermen.

INDIA: (*Plinking sheet of paper with index finger*) More at 4.30, I see.

BIMBO: I know, I know. (*Pause.*) I say, do I really have to see the GOC *and* the Chief Con this afternoon?

INDIA: Of course you do.

BIMBO: It's too hot. Far too hot.

INDIA: That palmhouse was simply stifling this morning.

BIMBO: One of my better speeches, I thought. At least they can grow their own pineapples now. I told his mayorship that but he was not amused – 'Would anyone want a Belfast pineapple? I ask ye?' Couldn't at all see the uses of pineapples. (*Sniffs.*) The scent of pollen is on the air / I . . . (*About to sneeze*) am growing . . . FEVER (*Sneezing loudly*) -ISH! (*Gesturing*) Shut the window, sweety.

INDIA: (*Bored and casual*) I hardly think I came all the way over here to shut windows. (*Pauses.*) But here goes. (*Gets up slowly and crosses room.*) Voilà! (*Shuts window.*) I have done my duty.

8

BIMBO: (*Feigning annoyance*) If I hear that dreadful word uttered in this room once again – I'll (*Stubs cigarette out.*) scream very very loudly. 'Member what he said when he stood against her?

INDIA: Uh-uh.

BIMBO: (*Solemnly*) 'I believe it is my duty.' Not – (*Hectic*) I want it – I need it – I'm dying for it – give me – POWER! (*Languid*) Silly sod . . . pompous ass . . . ruthless bugger. And so this (*Waving at room*), this is power. The possibility of quiet in a world of noise. And here am I, miles from civilization, treading in the old boy's footsteps . . . across the sands of the Kalahari. Give me the FO, say I. Make me someone else. I simply want to be someone else.

INDIA: Quite. One feels oneself becoming an entirely different person over here. It always does strange things to me, crossing water. Just imagine, while you were waffling on in that muggy palmhouse this morning I kept eyeing this lovely big councillor chap – you know the sort? – black box spectacles and a C & A blazer. Shiny buttons and a really obese Windsor knot. There was something awfully chunky about him. It's like this craving for junk food I get – just can't shake it off.

(*Goes over to window, printer starts.*)

BIMBO: Should've dropped an artichoke on his crotch.

INDIA: Remind me. Next time we're in City Hall. (*Staring out of window*) Herby must have turned the sprinklers on. It looks delicious out there on the lawns.

(*Printer stops.*)

BIMBO: If you ask me – and no one ever does – those lawns are rather less than cost effective.

INDIA: (*Walking back to desk*) Well, if one considers that airport at Port Stanley . . .

BIMBO: Don't! I can't bear to think of all the concrete they poured in – probably feed it to the bloody kelpers. A thousand plastic Portakabins round the perimeter – each one stuffed with a young squaddy doing macramé, only pausing to fart every five minutes. And the wind blows – non-stop.

9

D'you know what they've named it? – Turf Lodge? Ask the Gook.

INDIA: Funny the sprinklers out there when it rains so much.

BIMBO: (*To himself*) Mind you, we've oodles of lovely rhododendrons, (*Muses, donnish.*) beeches . . . chestnuts . . . Bloody silly ducks too.

INDIA: I absolutely detest those ducks.

BIMBO: One has to laugh every time the helicopter drops.

INDIA: Bloody scares 'em, bloody ducks.

BIMBO: Nice, very nice, the way the Chinks do 'em. I recall this banquet – was it Hong Kong? – no, not Hong Kong. . . . Hall of a Thousand something or other. All that Mou-Tai and oysters and lovely lovely duck.

INDIA: Fuck off, they said.

BIMBO: Well, they would, wouldn't they? Not that I'd put it quite so bluntly (*Mimics.*) speakin' personlly like. (*Phone rings as he speaks.*)

INDIA: Chinese Laundry here. (*Listens, frowns, puts phone down.*)

BIMBO: Anyone?

INDIA: No one. (*Moving to window*) It's simply stifling in here. (*Opens window.*)

BIMBO: (*Reaching for model airplane, fiddling with decal*) No, they didn't, the Chinks – put it in quite so many words. But it was damned sight hotter than this hole. Fed well, though – good scoff, good bottle, lots of blossomy avenues and palaces. It all went terribly terribly smoothly. Business as usual. (*Lands plane.*)

INDIA: Well, I wasn't invited. Before my time.

BIMBO: Yes–yes. (*Lights cigarette.*) Only thing I ever liked about Humphrey was his name.

INDIA: Oh, sod him. I'll never forget the day the phone rang. The thirteenth of September!

BIMBO: Packing to go to Paris of all places!

INDIA: I'll swear, d'you know what he said? – (*Mimics.*) – 'the word is Belfast'. I don't think I've ever been so disappointed in my entire life.

BIMBO: Nonsense, my dear. I thought of my – well, duty. Had

to polish it damned hard I did. Tatiana, now – she didn't
like it one tiny bit. Turned very bloody. Said I could go out
on my own, she wouldn't open a solitary solitary jumble
for any of those ghastly people. So here I am – lying on my
back –

INDIA: (*With some spite*) And thinking of England.
(*Singing, noise of brush on balcony.*)
HERBY: (*Off*) I wish I wish,
　　　　　I wish in vain,
　　　　　I wish I were
　　　　　A maid again,
　　　　　But a maid again
(HERBY *peers in.*)
　　　　　I'll never be . . .
(*Enters.*)
BIMBO: (*Musing, to* INDIA) Duke Humphrey, now . . .
(*While* BIMBO *is talking* HERBY *looks at* INDIA *and mimics
putting a cigarette to his mouth. She nods and* HERBY *advances
to coffee table.*)
. . . I spent quite a slice of my life in that gloomy den.
HERBY: (*Giving both breast pockets a perfunctory pat*) Have you a
light on you, Bimbo?
BIMBO: Down there, silly – under the port wing.
(HERBY *picks up lighter.*)
Reach me one, would you? there's an angel.
(*Phone rings,* HERBY *lights two cigarettes, hands* BIMBO *one
and moves to window. Exit* HERBY.)
INDIA: (*Brisk*) Yes – 6.30 – he–is–quite–bye.
BIMBO: Anyone?
INDIA: The Gook. He's about to take off from somewhere up
north.
BIMBO: (*Looking at watch*) But you said 6.30 – it's not even
4 o'clock!
INDIA: (*With studied patience*) Chief Con 6.30 – the Gook arrives
with the Chamber of Commerce chappies at 4.30. Then
half-way through you and he take a photocall. You'll still
have enough time for a private meeting before the Chief
Constable arrives.

BIMBO: Oh yes, neat tack that. One doesn't on the one hand want to spend too long with the Gook – man's a dreadful bore – but on the other hand we do need to plan our little pincer movement beforehand. Chief Constable's a wily bird, I fear.
(*Sound of printer.*)

INDIA: So why look so miffed when I tell you? You specifically asked to see the General Officer Commanding on his own – memo. Before the joint official meeting – memo.

BIMBO: True–true, yes–yes. Of course I did. It's just one shivers to think of them, these soldier–scholars. They scribble their anal prose in cheap jotters, then lecture us – ye gods! on boring awful subjects like strategic planning.

HERBY: (*Sticking his head through window as he sweeps*) Ah, y're a terrible complainer, Bimbo.

INDIA: Nonsense, Herby, he enjoys it.

BIMBO: Back to your labours, dear boy. Some of us need space to contemplate. Liberty, Leisure, Privacy, say I.

HERBY: I *am* working – it's you that's lyin' about. Y'must've bedsores by now, Bimbo.

BIMBO: Now, now, Herbert, no sedition please.
(HERBY *turns his back and dusts a bay tree.*)
Just consider my vast and unrewarding labours – open a palmhouse here, press the flesh there . . . climb out of helicopters, (HERBY *moves out of sight.*) open leisure centres in places with names like (*Shudders*) Comber or . . . Lur*gan*. Then I have to issue the odd appeal for calm, sound out a few trusties, reward the bearers.
(*Gets up, hunched, and moves towards one of the closed windows, cups hands and shouts.*) BLOODY DUCKS!
(*Glances at printer.*)

INDIA: Oh, do be quiet, Bimbo, the Bennies'll hear you.

BIMBO: (*Tearing off print-out*) Don't care.

INDIA: And besides, Herby might think you're getting at him.

BIMBO: (*Stubborn, petulant*) Don't give a toss. Why, I'd just like to say how absolutely splendid my tour has been –

INDIA: (*Sprightly*) Of–course–my–wife–and–I –

BIMBO: (*Joining in, glumly*) look–back –

INDIA: On–our–three–years–here . . . (*Snaps fingers*) . . .
on–our–three–years–*there* –

BIMBO: (*Getting into the spirit*) There–in–that–quite–
delightful–corner–of–the–great–British–Commonwealth –

INDIA: With unmingled joy –

BIMBO: And–fondest–memories –

INDIA: (*Sugary*) They're–such–lovely–people . . . They're–
such–lovely–people.
(*Slight pause as* BIMBO *flops back on* chaise-longue *and*
INDIA *holds a saccharine pose.*)

BIMBO: God, I could do with a drink after that.

INDIA: Well, you can fetch it yourself. I'm exhausted.
(HERBY *passes back, oblivious, holding a small plant as if it's
an injured bird.*)

BIMBO: Herby!
(HERBY *disappears.*)
Herby! Why doesn't he come?

INDIA: (*Mimics*) Some of us have wurk t'do.

BIMBO: (*Musing*) Of course none of them has got anything that
even remotely resembles a trained mind. And just when one
thinks one's got them cornered (*Reaches out and feels idly for
model plane*) they start to lay down some awful barrage of
quite irrelevant flak and one has to very suddenly (*Lifts
plane*) do a sort of Lin Pao and get out quick.

INDIA: I've never known such people for –

BIMBO: (*Cutting in*) Names, dates, places – everywhere from
Ballyboley to Ballymuck. Out they bloody come. All quite
beside the point, of course. (*Lands plane.*)

HERBY: (*From balcony*) Are y'rantin' again, Bimbo? Y'never
quit.

BIMBO: Gyppy tummy, dear boy. That's the line I take. Look,
there should be a flask of Mercier in the fridge – d'you
think you could possibly stretch to opening it? We'll simply
have to fall back on the Brut if you can't find any.

HERBY: (*Entering slowly*) It's between you and your conscience,
Bimbo.

13

BIMBO: Oh, shut up.

INDIA: Herby, surely you can spot a storm cloud by now? Gingerly does it.

BIMBO: (*Lighting a cigarette,* HERBY *taking his time*) Aye, brother, Bimbo is not well the day – this special special day. (*Normal voice, slightly flustered.*) Bad enough being addressed by Herby – makes one feel like Harold Nicolson being dumped on by Ernie Bevin. But who on earth was Jim trying to kid? Those lovely bloody people! Who does he *need* to kid? Now? He got out, and now I'm here. It's quite incredible. Belfast is simply derelict – reminds me of Oran back in '62. Reminds me of Liverpool now.

INDIA: I thought you'd never been to Liverpool?

BIMBO: Nor have I, my dear. It's not the sort of place one actually *goes* to. One simply hears of it – like video hypermarkets, or the Third World. I believe the entire city is ringed with the most enormous rubbish dumps, and the unemployed have this pastime they practise there – gleaning, I believe it's called. And I tell you – Bimbo is a gleaner too. He picks things up (*Lifts plane*) and he puts things down. (*Drops plane.*) He scrapes the second-rate and the second-hand.

(HERBY *fetching glasses slowly.*)

It's all junk – junk food, junk people, junk roads, junk speeches, junk houses. I mean, look at those ghastly ghastly curtains – the sort of thing you find in some gross cheapo bungalow.

INDIA: I don't suppose you've ever actually been in a bungalow either?

BIMBO: Good God, no. Have you?

INDIA: (*Smiling*) Once upon a time with a sweet sweet boy I was.

BIMBO: Don't! please! I can't bear it! White lice – suburbs; grey lice – council. Let them fight it out in their little asphalt way. Now that we're done for as a great power it's crystal clear that the loss of possessions, the claim of the proles to be a privileged race – sloth, envy, and increasing poverty – have sunk us all. Soon we'll have a country divided up between proles and apparatchiks.

(*Champagne pops and* HERBY *grins as cork misses* BIMBO.)
Thank God for that!
(HERBY *silently hands* INDIA *a glass, then* BIMBO.)
To the *fine*, not the *mauvaise*, Herb – cupbearer, bringer of
bubbly, we pledge this toast.
(*All raise glasses, drink, then relax.*)
Of course the House is full of little boys from bungalows
these days.

HERBY: Is that right? Must be a real scunner for ye.

BIMBO: Estate agents, small-town solicitors, dentists – drip-dry
accountants with accents fine-tuned by British Leyland.

HERBY: Ack, it sounds desperate, Bimbo. It's a wonder y'stick it.

INDIA: Oh, but he doesn't. He simply doesn't.

BIMBO: (*Oblivious*) The *petit embourgoisement* of a once-great
party simply has to be seen to be believed. I never know how
one actually talks to them.

HERBY: Sure they listen to you, Bimbo.

BIMBO: There you're wrong, Herb. Take champagne now
(*Raises glass.*) – they don't drink it. Odd young fogey who's
into real ale, but some are even teetotal, I suspect. (*Raising
glass*) Ah, champagne – champagne is the right drink for
politics. It stimulates in the moment and does not deaden
afterwards. I tell them that, but back to their suburbs they
trog – unimpressed and unannealled.

HERBY: (*Leading him on*) At least you're safe over here, Bimbo.

BIMBO: Safe? Safe? You surely can't be serious? The Ulster
suburbs look every bit as awful . . . part of England's gift to
the twentieth century they are.

HERBY: Ah, you're a hard man.

BIMBO: Miles and miles of similar houses – moderate incomes,
moderate opinions, moderate achievements. The most
inspired mediocrity.

HERBY: (*Walking out on to balcony*) Ack you're awful savage,
Bimbo.

BIMBO: (*As if really annoyed*) And you're a bloody cave-dweller,
sweetie.

INDIA: Perhaps we could go over the text for this thingie now?
They're due at 4.30.

BIMBO: Due? Who?

INDIA: (*Through papers*) The commercials . . . Chamber of Commerce. You know.

BIMBO: Ah, the Samuel Smilers with the knivers. At least it's too early for some of their unspeakable ethnic food – not another (*Sags.*) Ulster fry.

INDIA: Well, I've popped in a nice quote from the Bible.

BIMBO: Good–good.

INDIA: (*Flicking a page up*) It's what's–his–name . . . (*Loses page.*) – oh piss! (*Finds it.*) – yes, 'as the gospel St Paul says' –

BIMBO: Apostle, honeybunch, not gospel.

INDIA: That's odd. Are you sure? I thought Jesus Christ had twelve gospels and they – you know – sort of followed him about the place.

BIMBO: Proceed, Salome.

INDIA: (*Huffy*) Well, I'm not going to ask who he was. (*Reading*) 'As the Apostle St Paul says, "Obey them that have the rule over you, and submit yourselves . . ." '

BIMBO: (*Clicking fingers*) Goody, but drop the 'saint' before Paul.

INDIA: (*Concentrating*) Right – ' "for they watch for your souls, as they that must give account, that they may do it with joy, and not with grief: for that is unprofitable for you".' OK?

BIMBO: OK, OK. Lovely definite article, them that have the rule over you. Maybe the gospel Paul was an Ulsterman? After all Homer was a woman, I'm told.

HERBY: (*Appearing with bay tree*) That's rubbish, Bimbo, and you know it.

BIMBO: Good quote, though.

HERBY: Aye, it's a grand quote. They'll really love that. (*Mimics.*) – The boy that larns that'll go far.

INDIA: (*Puzzled*) But Herby, I thought – you know – I thought you were a believer too?

HERBY: Aye, that's right, India – the gospel Herby. (BIMBO *sniggers.*)

INDIA: Oh, shut up, you two.

BIMBO: Glad we see eye to eye on something, Herb.

(HERBY *fills glasses*.)
You may be a bit bush in your manner sometimes, but you're a damned good bottle man.

HERBY: Cracked a few in my time, Bimbo.

BIMBO: Haven't we all, dear boy? (*Cranking himself up*) Must go for a jimmy. (*Exit*.)

HERBY: (*Lifting bay tree, propitiating*) Lovely smell that. Rich and dry. Rich and dry. I hear tell a leaf of this bakes real good in rice pudden.

INDIA: I simply can't imagine your cooking.

HERBY: (*Needled*) Nursery food – isn't that what yous uns call rice pudden? Bet y'never feed on that at yur big bankwits?

INDIA: None of your business what we're served.

HERBY: Artichokes? Aubergines? Sparragrass? It's their growin' I watch over. Warm and gentle, plants are. Aye, you eat them, but I grow them.

BIMBO: (*Entering briskly, buttoning flies*) Nonsense, Herby. Much as I admire your delicate horticultural skills you must know perfectly well that all our vegetables are flown in at huge expense by one of your friendly local airlines.
(*To* INDIA) Now, dear, I've just had a thought in the *pissoir* – we'd better gum something in about ideology – procrustean bed of theory, that sort of thing.

INDIA: (*Turning up another file*) I'll snip something out of one of your other speeches.

HERBY: (*Lifting bay tree out*) That's the trouble wi'you episcopals, Bimbo – no doctrine.

BIMBO: (*Gravely*) Sound and steady, dear boy. We didn't invent commonsense for nothing, you know. Yes, we work by the rules – and by *the* rule. (*Whistles* 'Rule Britannia'.)

HERBY: Knock it off, Bimbo, would ye? Y're a tuneless critter. (*Goes to window*.)

BIMBO: The rules, Herbert – we make them –

HERBY: Aye, and ye break 'em.
(*Knock on door,* HERBY *disappears, enter* NORMAN *with briefcase*.)

BIMBO: Ah Norman – grab your glass and read me my lines.

NORMAN: (*Sitting down and taking documents from briefcase*)

My point – I beg pardon – *your* point, Secretary of State –
(HERBY *peeks in and out while they talk.*)
is that we live on an island behind an island. And as this is
the first of a series of *major* speeches – speeches of
reassurance to the majority community – it would be
helpful to point out that the two major islands –

BIMBO: (*Impatiently*) Oh stop major-majoring me!

NORMAN: – that the two most important islands . . . and I am
not forgetting, and will specifically mention, Rockall – that
this group of islands forms an archipelago which in turn
forms a political sub-system. Britain has a permanent
interest in moderating the sub-system as a whole.

BIMBO: Why?

NORMAN: Eh, well, she just has.

BIMBO: Has she forsooth? I'd stuff bloody Rockall up Dublin's
bum if I got half a chance.

NORMAN: (*Continuing with prim firmness, sipping wine*) Northern
Ireland is not a political and administrative place apart –
rather it lies at the interface between the two sovereign
governments in the archipelago. Ireland on its own does not
have an intelligible –

BIMBO: (*Pointing*) Your drink, old chap –

NORMAN: (*Lifting glass*) – does not have an intelligible culture.

BIMBO: (*Smacking lips, drinking from Norman's glass*) Lovely
taste of cricket bats – hope you find that intelligible?

NORMAN: (*Continuing*) Yet both islands are open to all the winds
that blow. They illustrate the organic links within the
archipelago. My answer to the coercive irredentist dream
(*Standing up,* HERBY *peers in.*) is that in a world where 600
people a year die violently in Miami, 250 UK servicemen
die on the Falklands in six weeks, the one hundred or so
people a year who die violently in Northern Ireland fall into
perspective. My government's answer is therefore contained
in the articles of the Anglo-Irish Agreement, and in our
fervent commitment to Continuing Direct Rule.
(BIMBO *and* INDIA *slumping.*)
And Continuing Direct Rule is, I would solemnly affirm,
Permanent Direct Rule, Direct Rule for ever and ever. But

it is Direct Rule improved to give such rule a more indigenous flavour.

(INDIA *asleep*, BIMBO *snoring*.)

We need to support the production of Ulster painting, of Ulster music, and of Ulster poetry (Ulster drama, too, of course). No man, after all, is an island, and of the internal stability of the entire archipelago there can be no doubt whatsoever. (*Looks around pleased with himself*.)

INDIA: (*Half-asleep*) Get off . . . stop it . . . I'm bloody tired.

BIMBO: (*Waking*) God's sake, India, get someone to give you a hand job, would you?

(*Turning heavily to* NORMAN) Norman . . . I heard some of that – not much, but enough. Know what it was?

NORMAN: No, Secretary of State.

BIMBO: *Merde – Scheisse* – wind and total piss. Bloody terrible. If you think I'm going to get up on my hind legs and spout a load of bumf about dentists and irredentists, then you're round the sodding twist. Permanent Direct Rule indeed! Back to the Gold Standard you mean. It's not on, old fruit.

NORMAN: (*Sitting down*) But, Secretary of State, I'm given to understand . . .

BIMBO: You're not given to understand anything, chump. (*Starts to get up slowly, relapses*.) No, you can go. Over there . . . on your feet, man. *Jaldi, jaldi*, chop, chop. (NORMAN *gets up, looking startled*.)

There – in the corner. (*Pointing to escritoire*) Come on, bit of paper – there – take it out. Now – *habemas papam*. (*Patronizing*) That's right, unfold it. Good–good. Now – read.

NORMAN: (*Reading*) Politics and public administration have about them an Alice-in-Wonderland-like unreality. A system of government developed by a great nation has been imposed upon a province the size of Yorkshire. An imposing parliament has been built with administrative offices attached at an inconvenient distance from the town, and this in a province which could well be administered by a couple of commissioners and the normal machinery of local government. The government is in effect that of a loyalist dictatorship . . .

(*Noise of helicopter above audience, descending to land on lawn beyond balcony, curtains blow in.*)

. . . constituencies have been so devised . . .

BIMBO: (*To* INDIA *over noise*) Bloody Gook!

NORMAN: . . . as where possible to split the RC vote. There is virtually no opposition . . .

BIMBO: Norman, that piece of paper you clutch there in your hand is a mere nine years senior to Neville Chamberlain's. (*Starts to put shoes on.*)

NORMAN: I thought it was a bit out of date.

BIMBO: Only a trifle, Norm. And Mr Whoever-he-was goes on to call your lot an opinionated, volatile, materialistic, intensely provincial people, for ever in the grip of paranoia. Am I correct?

NORMAN: (*Glancing at paper*) Roughly speaking, those words do appear in this text.

BIMBO: (*Clicking fingers*) Give me it.

(NORMAN *hands* BIMBO *the first paper.*)

Nothing changes much in the island behind the island. (*Making paper into dart*) There.

(*Buzzer.*)

INDIA: Yes, yes.

(*To* BIMBO)

Delegation—delegation. Your reception is starting downstairs. The GOC is about to make an entrance.

BIMBO: Oh God! (*Slings dart at open window, it disappears.*) Out, Norman, out! Redraft and report back . . .

(*Detaining him*)

Hold on – on second thoughts you'd better come to this damned reception . . . Off you go and warm them up, then slip out and redraft pronto.

(*Exit* NORMAN.)

Bloody commercials!

HERBY: (*Entering, throwing crumpled dart at* BIMBO) Thought you preferred them plastic, Bimbo?

(*Printer starts, its buzzer rasps intermittently.*)

INDIA: Now, now, Herby, can't you see he's under pressure!

BIMBO: Bloody hell! switch that damned machine off!

HERBY: Ack, Bimbo, wise up – y'cannie switch it off.

BIMBO: I'd like to blow the damned thing up. (*Still putting shoes on.*)

INDIA: (*Tearing off print-out*) Hardly concerns us – Home Secretary – ground rules – plastic baton rounds in Britain. That's mainland.

HERBY: Aye, that's mainland all right.

INDIA: (*Quickly*) Shut up – look (*To* BIMBO) – can't be a mistake, can it?

(HERBY *glancing at papers on her desk.*)

No, damned buzzer.

BIMBO: (*Squinting, buzzer stops*) Can't make it out.

INDIA: Says the pound's only worth fifty cents now.

BIMBO: (*Uninterested*) Suppose it's got to be worth something . . . Hold the fort, my dear. I go to console the commercials below. And Herby you really ought to go out and at least do a spot of pretend horticulture. (*Moving to door.*)

HERBY: OK, Bimbo, I'll see you this evenin'. (*Moving to window.*)

INDIA: (*Still staring at print-out*) Incredible! Absolutely incredible! Two pounds for a dollar! It's collapsing!

ACT TWO

Ten minutes later. INDIA *crouched on* chaise-longue *with phone.*
She speaks in an altered, urgent, snappy voice.

INDIA: . . . Martin? . . . Right . . . Martin? – God, I've been
trying to catch you all over the place.
Well, that's a relief. Look, this is straight from the horse's
mouth. But it's your friendly untouchable brings it you –
comprenne?
Sure–sure. The word is – or the words are – fork-tongue.
Yes, I'll graipe away, darling, never fear.
What's the policy say, then? – in capital letters, Slippery
Slope, Hit Temple, Stand Firm, Pledge Reassurance,
Fervent Hope, Slip-Slip, Double Distance.
You don't understand! Well, think about it.
Look, love, the fine print on the policy reads – separation,
divorce, alimony. And the alimony will be paid in dollars –
right, dollars. You'll be better off than we are.
Oh, haven't you heard? There's a run on sterling. It's heavy
. . . yes, very heavy.
Yes–Yes – goodbye to the Union . . . virgin once again . . .
short way to Tipperary . . .
Yep. All that guff.
Sure–sure. Bye!
(*She puts phone down, sits still, gets up and goes into pantry.*
HERBY *stalks in, looking for a cigarette.* INDIA *enters and*
moves to desk.)
Oh, hello Herby. (*Sits down, pushes keyboard.*) I thought his
majesty had banished you to the gardens?
HERBY: Huh, know what they call that ould weed-patch now?
INDIA: (*Abstracted, pressing keyboard*) Oh damn! (*Pressing*
keyboard again, silence.)
HERBY: (*Annoyed*) I ast ye a question, India.
INDIA: (*Still concentrating*) Oh, did you? what was it?
HERBY: (*Going over to her, pointing and speaking firmly*) I said

22

d'you know what they call that . . . that garden now?

INDIA: I haven't the slightest idea.

HERBY: They call it the Garden of Gethsemane.

INDIA: Oh, do they? Rather a sweet name for it, don't you think?

HERBY: D'you know what happened there?

INDIA: (*Puzzled*) No, why on earth should I?

HERBY: Why should ye! I'll tell ye . . . (*Shrugging*) ack, what's the use? Gospel spoons, gospel spoolies . . . mention Judas t'you lot and ye's think he's some kinda pop singer!

INDIA: Herby, Herby, I can't bear it when you talk like that. You really are so very very bush.

HERBY: Aye, the burnin' bush, that's Herby.

INDIA: (*Raising one hand*) Don't! Enough! Look, this silly machine's stuck. Can you fix it for me?

HERBY: I can not.

INDIA: What d'you mean you can't?

HERBY: What I said, India – I can't fix no machines. Specially a spacer like thon thing.

INDIA: (*Huffy*) Call yourself a man!

HERBY: Nah, just call me ignorant.

INDIA: Oh, you're that all right.

HERBY: God, y're one t'talk! (*Mimics.*) 'Didn't Jesus Christ have twelve gospels and they – you know – sort of followed him about the place?'

INDIA: Will you shut up! You impossible bloody bog man! (*Pushing keyboard, tearful*) My magic apple's glitched! It's simply chewing up files!

HERBY: (*Moving towards her*) I dunno, India – 'tisnae my necka th'woods. Things made a'metal – cars, like, motorbikes – aye – same wi' guns – they're all the same t'me. I don't touch 'em, don't work wi' 'em. I only like growin' things.

INDIA: (*Stiffly*) I can just see you in rope sandals.

HERBY: (*Puzzled*) Rope? What d'ya mean, rope? Sandals?

INDIA: God, Herby, you're *so* provincial.

HERBY: Aye, well, I can't help that. I was never outa the narth. Been here all m'life I have.

INDIA: Poor you. (*Tapping keyboard*) Oh, damn this thing!

23

HERBY: (*Leaning over keyboard*) Maybe if y'pushed that un?

INDIA: (*Trying*) Nope.

HERBY: That'n there?

INDIA: (*Pressing, sceptical*) Oh marvellous! How wonderful! (*Abstractedly hugging him*) You're such a pet!

(HERBY *moves on to balcony*, INDIA *without noticing continues working keyboard.*)

. . . this is really super! . . . you've a hidden talent, Herby, really you have . . . don't tell me you're not pleased . . . Herby? (*Looks round.*) Herby? (*Printer starts.* INDIA *goes over to it, glances briefly at print-out, goes thoughtfully to balcony.*) Herby! . . . I'm just going to get a coffee, d'you want one?

(*Goes to pantry.* HERBY *appears but doesn't enter.* INDIA *enters with one cup and Cona coffee jug.*)

Oh there you are. (*Apprehensive.*) I wondered where you'd disappeared to. Here, d'you want a coffee?

(HERBY *shrugs.*)

What's got into you, then? C'mon tell me.

HERBY: (*Stubborn*) Nothun.

INDIA: Don't be silly. Here, (*Pours coffee, hands it to him.*) take this.

(*Goes into pantry, comes back with another cup*, HERBY *swallows his coffee and hands cup back.*)

HERBY: Here.

INDIA: What on earth's bugging you? I don't know what I've done to deserve this.

HERBY: Aye, well, neither do I.

INDIA: I mean I thanked you – thanked you ever so nicely – when you showed me how to work that silly computer. I did, didn't I?

HERBY: You did, sure.

INDIA: Well then?

HERBY: Well nothun.

INDIA: Oh God, I know, I know –

HERBY: (*Entering*, INDIA *moves back*) No, y'don't.

INDIA: Yes, I do!

HERBY: You do not.

24

INDIA: (*Putting cups down on table*) Look, just because I called you a pet there's absolutely no need to get all huffy like that. (*Voice quavering slightly*) I didn't mean what you thought I meant. I didn't.

HERBY: (*Raising hands in wounded gesture*) Ack, India . . . I may be just, like, I mean, a wee man stuck here wi' no big knowledge nor nothun – a fella that has t'go below and stick pot plants in that there room, like a servant just . . . but I have m'feelings same as –
(*They clinch.*)

INDIA: (*Softly*) I wasn't thinking, love. I wasn't. You're not a pet at all.
(*She rubs against him and kisses him. They manoeuvre to* chaise-longue.)
You're such a lovely lovely man . . . crumbly, really crumbly. Delicious.

HERBY: (*Watching door*) An' y're . . . y're like this pieca light at's come down t'this wee spatta earth . . . 'n blessed it. Aye. (*More action.*)

INDIA: Oh, I love the way you talk. I love it. (*Stroking his nose with one finger*) You must never feel hurt – never.

HERBY: (*Sighing, hugging her*) Ack, India . . .

INDIA: And I don't know why you go on so, as if you really believe you're stupid.

HERBY: (*With glum sincerity*) But I am. I know I am.

INDIA: No, you're not. You know all sorts of things – things I've never heard of.

HERBY: Ack, I'm awful thick like.

INDIA: Well, I don't think so.

HERBY: Sure I heard y'there now – on the phone – talkin' 'bout some temple. A temple! Jees, that's beyond me. And big words y'were sayin' – like alimoanie . . .

INDIA: Alimony.

HERBY: Aye, alimony. Alimony. But then I thought just . . . I thought 'bout thon temple . . . ack, no. I'm wrong.

INDIA: (*Snuggling*) How can you be wrong when you haven't even told me what you thought?

HERBY: Just . . . I'm bound t'be.

INDIA: No, you're not. Go on, tell me. (*No answer.*) Oh, go on, please. (*She kisses fingers on his right hand.*)

HERBY: Ack, it's hard, like. I mean . . . sure y'won't laugh at me, will yu?

INDIA: (*Snuggling*) Course I won't, silly.

HERBY: I mean, I read one time – read in a newspaper like – 'bout this temple – a golden temple, they have in . . . in thon place y're named for . . . n'India.

INDIA: (*Brightening*) Go on.

HERBY: Well, didn't, didn't – it was a good while back – didn't that womun 'at got shot –

INDIA: Mrs Gandhi, yes –

HERBY: Aye, Mrs Gandhi – didn't she send the troops inta that there golden temple?

INDIA: (*Giving him big hug and kiss*) Mm, you *are* getting warm.

HERBY: (*Loosening*) Aye, I'm warm all right.

INDIA: Go on, you big gorgeous man.

HERBY: Well, then, I says t'myself – Herby, thon temple – thon temple – is it Derry or is it Portiedown?

INDIA: Oh, those little towns are all the same to me!

HERBY: (*With apparent innocence*) Is that right now, India?

INDIA: But (*Impressed*) you've said something terribly, terribly sharp.

HERBY: Ack, no – sure I'm only guessin'.

INDIA: Well, what would you guess is going to happen? (*Hugs him.*)

HERBY: Now . . . (*More action.*) . . . dunno.

INDIA: Oh, go on – guess.

HERBY: Sure all that's for politicians. I know nothun 'bout all that.

INDIA: Come on, guess.

HERBY: I can't. I just can't. (*Strokes her hair.*)

INDIA: Just a teeny teeny bit – then I'll tell you.

HERBY: Ah, sure y'd better not tell me nothun.

INDIA: Oh I will, I will. But promise me – promise you won't breathe a word – to anyone.

HERBY: Oh no, never. I wouldni do that, love. (*Pause.*) I wonder, like, y'could even say that?

INDIA: I'm only teasing, silly. You know I trust you.

HERBY: Aye, well . . .

INDIA: Go on – guess.

HERBY: Well . . . it's hard, but. Still, I'd say it's like what allus happens this tima year now. I mean, there's the Orangemen marchin', (INDIA *nods*.) and Bimbo, he throws the soldiers at them – does it every year he does. So, like there's nothun new . . . Portiedown's the Golden Temple. That's all. Every July, it's hit. But this July – maybe, it's gonna be a bit diffrent, I reckon. A brave bit diffrent?

INDIA: (*Drawling*) Yeah, you got it.

HERBY: (*Puzzled*) Have I? I feel a bit lost like. I mean – seems like yu were leakin' info soon as Bimbo's back was turned.

INDIA: You think so?

HERBY: Well . . .

INDIA: Don't worry about his lordship. But you're right about the other thing.

HERBY: Ack, I am not!

INDIA: Mm, you are. It's going to be different – very different – this time round. (*Lying back with her head in his lap*) The whole idea's really very simple – darling Bimbo is talking about that little town that's the same as Derry – Londonderry. Right?

HERBY: Aye, right.

INDIA: And that other place you mentioned –

HERBY: Portiedown –

INDIA: Right, Porteedown. He says he wants to make them exactly the same.

HERBY: How's that now?

INDIA: You know . . .

HERBY: Jesus, I know nothun, India. Honest.

HERBY: Well, he says he's going to send them –

HERBY: Who's *them?*

INDIA: The Paras, silly – send them in salivating, he says –

HERBY: Sure, what's new 'bout that? He throws 'em in 'gainst th'Orangemen every July now.

INDIA: Ah, but I believe they did something just a teeny bit naughty years and years ago – in Londonderry, wasn't it?

HERBY: (*Sitting up*) O God! – Jesus! I see it all now! Bloody
Sunday! Twice over! He won't, will he!

INDIA: It's really rather neat, don't you think? I imagine Dublin
will lodge a strong protest on behalf of all those murdered
innocent Orange chappies – we're banking on a body count
of about twenty.

HERBY: Y'are? Oh God!

INDIA: Oh, don't be so sentimental. It's policy, policy.

HERBY: Jesus, he's a cunnin' hallion, Bimbo.

INDIA: Clever? Oh, for sure he's clever. *And* he's got something
else up his sleeve –

HERBY: He has, has he?

INDIA: Mm . . . couple of days before the do he wants me to
float a rumour about passports.

HERBY: 'Bout passports!

INDIA: Yes, you see there's a million bloody white South
Africans with blue passports. The British people don't want
them *and* this lot here flooding in – scary, scary . . . you
know. We're simply going to take them away.

HERBY: Ack, I've never had a passport in m'life, India, I
wouldn't know 'bout them things.

INDIA: Get yourself one, darling. Better green than blue I'd say
– *and* give me a lovely long kiss. (*Snuggling*) All being well,
Bimbo and I should be out of here by the end of July . . .
so we haven't much time to enjoy ourselves . . . we haven't
much time.

ACT THREE

The narrow strip of stage in front of the dropped curtain. Portrait of Queen Mother against the middle of the curtain. Right a low dais with lectern, left a sawn-off drinks table with a white linen tablecloth, glasses, bottles, ice bucket, a bunch of roses in a vase. BIMBO *pacing stiffly – waiting for audience to return after interval – holding his speech like a baton and whacking it on to the palm of his other hand.* BERNI, *the photographer, sits in front row of stalls. Enter* NORMAN *leading* HENDERSON *over dais.* HENDERSON *is dressed in a bottle-green sports blazer, blue slacks and brown suede shoes. He has a gin and tonic in one hand. He is middle-aged, well built, has shiny skin and grey hair. He appears honoured and anxious.*

NORMAN: Secretary of State, I know you're just about to start –

BIMBO: (*With a formal stiffness*) We really have run on much too long already.

NORMAN: – but I wonder if –

BIMBO: I've to chair a most important meeting this evening, you know.

NORMAN: – but I wonder if I could just quickly introduce –

HENDERSON: (*Pushing in and offering hand*) Ken Henderson. I'm very pleased to meet you again, sir. It's always a great honour indeed, t'meet you, sir . . . t'meet you.

BIMBO: (*In a grave voice, barely taking his hand*) Good evening, Mr Anderson.
(NORMAN *whispers.*)
. . . I mean, Henderson.

HENDERSON: (*Unctuous and confidential*) I just wanted to say, sir, that we're very grateful to you. Very grateful. There's been differences, I know.

BIMBO: *Local* difficulties.

HENDERSON: Yes, (*Puzzled*) local. But now I for one accept all your pledges 'bout the Union. Y'have my full confidence. And if I could just say, sir, that's quite something for an

29

Ulsterman to give to anyone. Oho yes, it's quite something.

BIMBO: I am sure it is.

(NORMAN *moves to talk to* BERNI, *the photographer*.)

I can assure you that feeling of confidence is entirely reciprocated.

HENDERSON: I'm very glad to hear you say that, sir. I just thought I had to tell you.

(*Flashgun*.)

There's . . . there are hundreds who wouldn't, though they'd think it – yes, and feel it to.

BIMBO: I much appreciate your speaking for them. And now –

(*Turning to dais*.)

HENDERSON: (*Credulous*) You do? I'm very glad. I am indeed. But tell me, sir, I've often wondered this – tell me, d'you like it here? Isn't the countryside – isn't it very – very attractive?

BIMBO: Oh yes, I adore it. A simply delightful spot.

HENDERSON: (*Flattered*) It is, isn't it? De-lightful. It's a great wee place. And the people, sir?

(*Enter* HERBY *carrying a pair of pot plants*.)

Tell me, how d'you find us?

BIMBO: (*Looking at dais*) Lovely people too. Ulstermen, finest in the world I often say – privately, of course.

HENDERSON: Oh yes, I understand, sir. You have to keep it private. Mind you, sir, there are some bad ones (*Looking quickly over shoulder*) waiting in the wings. They'd push me off the board if they got half a chance.

(HERBY *disposes pot plants on dais, then exits*.)

BIMBO: (*Automatically, still eyeing dais*) Your firm is making a good profit, I trust?

HENDERSON: (*Puzzled*) Firm? What firm? I mean, I have my own business, and that's going fine, sir. But the board here's different. I mean, we don't aim to make money, sir –

BIMBO: (*Almost interested*) How very Irish!

HENDERSON: (*Astonished*) Irish! Irish? but this is Ulster. You're in Northern Ireland, sir.

BIMBO: I am aware of *that*.

HENDERSON: Well, we're the same as you then.

(*Enter* NORMAN *near dais.*)

BIMBO: Perhaps you are. And perhaps you could explain to me how you can sit on a board of directors and not aim to make a profit? That strikes me as being a shade odd – a shade, well, Irish.

HENDERSON: (*Puzzled*) But . . . but. But, sir, we're – we're voluntary – we . . .

(BIMBO *turns to find* NORMAN *and taps him with speech.*)

BIMBO: Permanent Secretary, we seem to be in some slight difficulty about language here. I wonder if you'd care to interpret for me? (*Whispers in* NORMAN'S *ear.*)

NORMAN: I quite understand, Secretary of State.

(*Whispers in* BIMBO'S *ear,* BIMBO'S *face drops, he twists his speech.*)

BIMBO: (*Turning to* HENDERSON *with forced self-assurance*) My dear Henderson, it appears I may be in error. I thought for one tiny moment you'd come here as a representative from some Chamber of Commerce.

HENDERSON: Oh no, sir. No – this is the Eastern Health and Social Services Board. (*Gesturing at audience*) That's what we are.

BIMBO: Yes, yes, of course you are. And a fine job you're doing too. If you'll just excuse me. (*Leading* NORMAN *left*) Good God, man – I'm in quangoland! I can't give this speech. What on earth am I going to say?

NORMAN: (*Smiling faintly*) Couldn't you, well, change it as you go along? There must be some parts that still pertain to the good people gathered here?

BIMBO: Get me a very large vodka. (*To* HENDERSON) Awfully sorry, Whitehall on the blower you know. I simply had to take some advice.

HENDERSON: Yes, yes, I quite understand, sir. It must be terrible the responsibility you carry.

BIMBO: Oh dreadful! dreadful! I seem to work twenty hours every day, seven days a week.

HENDERSON: That *is* hard work, sir.

BIMBO: No, it's simply one's duty.

NORMAN: (*Offering tumbler*) A glass of water, Secretary of

State, before you speak?

BIMBO: Thank you. (*Swallows it in one gulp.*) And now –

(HENDERSON *latches on to his arm.*)

HENDERSON: It's very good to meet you, sir . . .

    (NORMAN *assists* BIMBO *on to dais, enter the* GOOK *who briskly moves* HENDERSON *out of the way as* BERNI *snaps* BIMBO, *then snaps the* GOOK *and* BIMBO *standing together smiling.*)

BIMBO: (*Leaning over to* NORMAN) Prompt me if I dry.
    (*Smooths ruffled speech on to lectern, takes out spectacle case and puts on reading glasses.*) Ladies and gentlemen (*Stops and peers over reading glasses which he deploys at moments during speech*) perhaps if I may I should first welcome you to a room which, much as I love and admire it – for its gracious furnishings, its quite superb view of the grounds of this noble mansion – is a room I nevertheless feel in all fealty isn't quite mine to roam around in. And for one very good reason I may say. This room (*Gesturing*) is as some of you will know Her Majesty the Queen Mother's very favourite room, and the furnishings in it owe much to her most distinguished taste and to her finer judgement. And I know the Queen Mother – who has stayed here many many times – agrees with what someone just now remarked to me, and that is that Ulster – Northern Ireland – is as the phrase so felicitously has it 'a great wee place'. Yes, a great wee place, a place that must always have a special esteem in English hearts. And what better way of translating that phrase so beloved of the classical poets – *amor loci* – as a–great–wee–place? It is a place for which I as an Englishman am most truly grateful. (*Pause as he fiddles and fusses with text and puts one hand in jacket pocket.*)

    Now, I had . . . I had intended to say a few words this evening about commerce, about fiscal policy, investment, incentive – that sort of thing. I know that some of you are in business, but others of you are not – some of you are lawyers, others teachers, and quite a few of you are, well, retired. So I thought that instead of talking about the economic life of this province I would do something which

it's been in my mind for a long time now to do – and that is
. . . (*Pause, fiddles.*) . . . and that is – well, simply as it
were to muse – yes, muse – on what it means to be in
government. Yes, (*Shuffles papers.*) government. But first
let me say that I agree very much with what St Paul says:
'Obey them that have the rule over you and submit
yourselves, for they watch for your souls, as they that must
give account, that they may do it with joy, and not with
grief: for that is unprofitable for you.' I'm sure all of us
gathered here in this room today will agree with those
words of apostolic wisdom.

Now we in England are perhaps too prone to fight shy of
ideas and so I would like just now to raise one or two ideas
and set them before you. Of course, it's one thing to
distrust – and rightly to distrust – the procrustean bed of
theory, but quite another to refuse ever to engage with an
idea. And it is precisely for that reason that I feel it my duty
– yes, duty – to air and reflect on some of the very
profound emotions to which this room gives rise. It is
because we are here – here in the Queen Mother's very
favourite room – is it not a lovely–lovely room? – that I
thought it might not be improper for me to discuss as it
were the relationship – yes, relationship – between
government and our great monarchy. Here I'm referring
not so much to, ah, sovereignty – for we all know that
Parliament is absolutely sovereign – but to the connection
between government and monarch. And that connection is
made – quite simply in my view – by the family, and I
mean any family. For the family is a small social unit which
shares – shares with civil society – the singular quality of
being non-contractual, and of arising – both for the
children and for the parents – of arising not out of choice
but out of natural, as it were, necessity. Now for the
majority of Englishmen the bond of family is a bond of
allegiance which has – well, it has immediate – and I mean
immediate – authority, because the family is something far
far greater than the mere sum of its members. And that
authority is the authority of tradition. So – to put it plainly,

33

if I may – an Englishman's loyalty to his monarch requires many things . . . ceremony, custom, a transcendental legitimacy, an established code of deference, *and* obedience (*Wagging finger*) – oh yes, obedience – obedience to the law of the land. The Englishman believes in historical vitality and in – in – the individual's sense of his society's will to live. And so when I speak of the Englishman's sense of that will and of his deep sense of fellowship with the social order, I am saying that this quite obviously cuts through any kind of dogma about so-called natural rights. Let us hear less of rights and more of duties, say I.

(*Looking at speech*) Now I've been – and I do hope you'll forgive me – a trifle reflective . . . a trifle, well, philosophical – but it is my very pleasant duty to now pay tribute to the work of . . . the work of the Eastern . . . (NORMAN *nods*.) . . . the Eastern Health and Social Services Board. And I would like to thank them for the many very energetic moves they have made to privatize some of the . . . eh (NORMAN *makes 'A'-sign by inverting two fingers and crossing them with one finger*.) ancillary services which our hospitals have to offer. Their motto is . . . (NORMAN *touches vase of flowers*.) . . . their motto is Funerals, Fast Food and Flowers. Privatize these and you are well on your way to a more efficient health service. I would also like to thank the Board for in the last year closing three hospitals –

NORMAN: (*Prompting*) Five!

BIMBO: I beg pardon, for closing *five* hospitals . . . eh (*Turning to* NORMAN) old people's homes?

NORMAN: Eleven.

BIMBO: (*Airily*) And for getting rid of eleven old people's homes.

NORMAN: *Sixteen* day-care centres.

BIMBO: (*With enjoyment*) Also – splendid this – for wiping sixteen quite unnecessary day-care centres off the map. And as I now recall the Board has been instrumental in effectively deunionizing the ambulance drivers throughout this great province. To the shroud-wavers, to those who would seek to delve yet again into Kincora, I say thank goodness for commensense, thank goodness for the Board – God bless the Board and all who sail in her!

ACT FOUR

SCENE I

A few minutes later. INDIA *stretched sleepily on* chaise-longue.
HERBY *perched on balcony opposite open middle window, smoking,
a glass of wine beside him. Printer starts. Enter* BIMBO *with*
AUSTIN (*the* GOC *or* GOOK). *Some hollow back-slapping, some
genuine relief.* INDIA *leaps up, looking slightly guilty, and
disappears into bathroom.* HERBY *snatches his glass and drops out of
sight immediately they enter.* AUSTIN *is athletic, trim like a squash-
player, and dressed casually in a military sweater, open-necked shirt
and green slacks. He is cold-eyed and vigilant, and his rare smiles
have a chalky, premeditated quality. His voice has an introspective,
slightly boyish tone. At all times he appears to be aware of his
surroundings professionally, like a carpet-fitter or an architect. This
shows in the measuring, disdainful look he turns on people and
things. Often he appears not to be listening, and when he speaks he
seems sometimes to be addressing another person.*

BIMBO: My very own personal snatch squad! – thank God you
  got me out of that mob! (*Pointing to chair*) My dear Austin,
  pray be seated, do.
AUSTIN: Very heavy those chaps. More like bodyguards than
  quango-quacks. (*Sitting down*) You smelt the thunder?
BIMBO: (*Glancing at printer*) Henderson the rain king – he's
  juju. Every time I stop to parley with him the drums start
  up. (*Beats chest.*)
  Boom-daboum! Boom-daboum! Notice how he tried to crowd
  into our little photocall?
AUSTIN: A vain chap. Ingratiating. Very.
BIMBO: Austin, we'll need to mark him. (*Scrumples print-out.*)
AUSTIN: I know Henderson – inside and out.
BIMBO: Good–good.
  (INDIA *appears with drinks.*)
INDIA: The Chief Constable will be here in thirty minutes,
  gentlemen.
BIMBO: Copperbottom cometh, Austin. (*Tosses crumpled paper in*

36

wastebin.) We really ought to have a word before he gets here. (*To* INDIA) Bloody cock-up you made!

INDIA: How me? What am I supposed to have done?

BIMBO: (*Pointing down*) That wasn't a damned bloody Chamber of Commerce!

INDIA: (*Realizing*) Oh no!

BIMBO: Oh yes.

INDIA: Not the . . . ?

BIMBO: Oh, some damned health board . . . never mind. Bimbo did his bumbling best. (*Clicking fingers*) Where's that file? (*She brings it.* BIMBO *puts on reading glasses and scans it while feeling for a cigarette*.)

M'yes . . . yes . . .

(INDIA *lights his cigarette*.)

You see, to be perfectly candid, Austin, they're getting a bit restless on the mainland. Even jumping Jack Hackett's gone ape . . . started writing silly letters to *The Times* 'bout a total pull-out. *Mail* and the *Sun* aren't as sound as they were. *Mirror* always was a damned nuisance. Trouble is, every day-dawn the natives scan our rags over their tea-cups. Gives them ideas.

(INDIA *hands out red plate of vol-au-vents*.)

AUSTIN: Ideas? We can't have that. (*Gets up, paces*.) I've always said we should be able to tell the press exactly where to get off. Fence 'em all up in Wapping, I say. There's never the same problem with judges, I find.

BIMBO: True–true. (*Stubbing cigarette out*) It's fine in principle, of course – usually a trifle dicey putting it into practice, though.

AUSTIN: I don't see why. You must let me explain the theory some day.

BIMBO: (*Raising hand*) Austin, don't put pen to paper. Please. Not yet awhile. (*Pacing*) Now Hackett's joined the hacks one feels the scribblers are telling us all what to do. I'll say one thing for the police – they never write books.

AUSTIN: Too busy doing overtime, that lot.

BIMBO: (*Hand on shoulder*) Look, Austin, as I see it the main issue is quite simple – the Chief Constable's unhappy, and

37

so are his chaps. He needs reassuring. (*Handing plate*)
Here, try another.

AUSTIN: I've told him many times, (*Taking one*) I'll lend him
all the groundhogs he wants (*Biting, gesturing*) – pongos,
trackers, know-how, hardware (*Holding it up*) – good, this.
All he need do is put it in writing.

BIMBO: (*Looking up*) Leaks in the ceiling – he has his problems.
Dublin's breathing down his neck just now. You'll find out
– when you've been here a bit longer.

AUSTIN: (*Pacing*) Give me – give him – just half a dozen really
good trackers. Kalahari bushmen – best in the world. They
simply melt on the ground. We'd five of them in the last
show – flew them up to Muscat before we took the Jebal.

BIMBO: Melt they may, but what on earth would we do with
them afterwards? Abandon them in a wildlife park
somewhere near Birmingham?

AUSTIN: What d'you do with all your supergrasses?

BIMBO: Oh we simply crate them off to the Costa Brava.
(*Confidential, motioning to chair*) Now look, Austin, what
I'm saying is that our chaps – *your* chaps – really ought to
drop back a shade. I mean, of course, a shade more. Slip
back into the shadows and lie doggo. I call it . . . (*Clicking
fingers*) I call it – damn, what is the bloody term?

INDIA: (*Not looking up from file*) Double-distancing, sweetie.

BIMBO: Yes, quite right, double-distancing. That's the name on
the policy, get it?

AUSTIN: (*Shrugging*) Well . . .

BIMBO: You see it's a bit like a satellite signal – we're
bouncing part of it off Dublin now. And the Cabinet
approves – it passed on the nod. So Direct Rule
continues, but becomes rather less direct, even somewhat
– well – indirect. That means that you and I can simply
keep our heads down. After all, police know the terrain,
know the natives – are the bloody natives. And if you can
put a marker down between your lot and their part-time
squaddies – all the better. Of course we'll lend them
support –

AUSTIN: Yes, *lend* – that's what I said to him. All I ask from the

Chief Constable is a piece of paper. I must have something in writing.

BIMBO: Listen, Austin, he has to watch his back – *and* think of Dublin. Won't put his name to anything with yours on it. That lets us off – and out. D'you see.

AUSTIN: Frankly I don't.

BIMBO: But we do need – and I mean *need* – a low profile. We're all having to slice the salami very very fine just now. It seems there just isn't enough cash to go round. Why shovel it into a stinking bog? *They* can give the blood –

AUSTIN: We'll keep the treasure. Fine. If you can't go in right to the hilt, (*Smashing hand into palm*) then you just have to drop back. Simple strategy, that's all.

BIMBO: Quite. Otherwise they're on the high ground and you're half-way down. It's a nonsense. India, what d'you say – why don't we let that nice little lord mayor of yours go ahead and twin with Durban? They could run the whole show on krugerrands and save us a bloody fortune.

INDIA: I hardly think that's *prektikal*.

AUSTIN: Oh, I don't know – I'd be sure to get my bushmen then.

BIMBO: But, Austin, you wouldn't be here any longer! That's the whole point!

AUSTIN: Oh, wouldn't I? Still I could advise them – for my usual fee. Send the trackers in first for a good sniff, then go in hard – *bang! bang!* blow their bloody heads off. That'll settle it. (*Printer.*)

BIMBO: (*Moving slowly to printer, affecting interest*) Muscat was good value, I hear?

AUSTIN: Poor prog . . . silly Sultan used to feed us this foul jelly. He shipped it in from Australia. God knows why.

BIMBO: Cure for crapulence, I suppose. You know, Austin, (*Looking up from print-out*) whenever I have a really bad hangover I always order up some pineapple and pickled herring – best cure I know. What d'you do?

AUSTIN: Oh, simply, run round the parade ground.

INDIA: How terribly active! I take a very hot bath then a vodka ice-cream.

BIMBO: Don't get many of those in the desert. (*Slowly scrumpling print-out as if disappointed, then binning it.*)

AUSTIN: You know what the desert is? – a fighting asset.

BIMBO: (*Nodding but bored*) I see – A Fighting Asset.

AUSTIN: Yes, damned useful. Like chucking bodies in an egg-timer. It turned them into pure sand, double-quick.

BIMBO: That Sultan of yours – chap who likes his Australian jelly – he didn't last very long, did he?

AUSTIN: Nope. One of his sons gave him the push.

INDIA: I suppose you can't go back now?

AUSTIN: (*Shocked*) Back to England you mean? I should hope I still can.

BIMBO: She means Muscat, silly.

AUSTIN: Of course I can. Go there all the time. I've got my own palace – didn't you know?

INDIA: Mm, all that lovely lovely sherbet.

BIMBO: I suppose you bathe in the stuff?

AUSTIN: Might do. Now and then.

BIMBO: (*Clapping hands together suddenly, decisively*) Jolly good! Lashings of sherbet pretty damned soon. That's it, dear boy. We're agreed.

AUSTIN: I suppose we must be. Remind me.

BIMBO: As I was saying – we hang out and we hang back – right back. They take the punishment, though we're always on call if things get really heavy. After all, a bootneck is not a policeman.

AUSTIN: Damned right he isn't.

BIMBO: And he is *not* a social worker.

AUSTIN: Enough said.

(HERBY *passes window half-concealed behind orange tree.*)
Who's he when he's at home?

BIMBO: God knows. He may sleep in a kennel for all I know.

INDIA: That's our very own gardener.

BIMBO: A simple soul. Mere child of nature. (*Gesturing*) Came with all this. I expect you've a team of them over in Lisburn.

INDIA: It's only Herby.

(*Printer, buzzer.*)

40

AUSTIN: (*Getting up*) Only? Only is lonely . . . (*Suspicious*) On his own sweet ownie own?

BIMBO: At ease, Austin, at ease. He's got his very own orange tree – keeps it in a little greenhouse somewhere behind the stables. Brings it up here sometimes for a bit of air and gracious living. Never fear – he's a trusty. (*Takes print-out.*)

AUSTIN: I take it you've read his file?

BIMBO: Course I have, dear boy. (*Looks at print-out.*) Nothing stuck, nothing sticky.

AUSTIN: He moved like a pongo.

BIMBO: Oh, Herby probably did a bit of soldiering in his day.

INDIA: Uh-uh. No, he didn't. He told me just now he'd never been out of this place in his life.

AUSTIN: (*Moving to window*) You're quite sure?

INDIA: Sure I'm sure. Oh he's terribly sweet and innocent and harmless. (*Phone rings,* INDIA *answers.*) Bit short notice, don't you think? . . . Yes, they are indeed waiting . . . very well . . . yes, I'll inform them. (*Replaces phone.*) The Chief Constable has been delayed.

BIMBO: Damn and blast!

AUSTIN: He really is trying to provoke me this time.

INDIA: Seems there's been a teeny spot of trouble somewhere – mortars, I believe she said.

AUSTIN: Newry again – I told them. RUC are very stupid.

INDIA: Perhaps. I couldn't pick up on it. Their speech is so very hard to follow.

BIMBO: (*Plinking print-out and grinning*) Bit nearer home than Newry. Thiepval – Lisburn – your own patch, Austin.

AUSTIN: Bloody hell! You must be joking! But you already knew! Here, what's it say?

BIMBO: (*Raising hand like policeman*) Seems they had a go at your lot for a change. That's all.

AUSTIN: I say, that's most unfair! I'd better scramble. (*Moves to door.*)

BIMBO: (*Restraining, handing print-out*) No, no, Austin. D'you see? – no blood on the floor, no casualties.

AUSTIN: Damn it, we've as good as got a treaty with the other lot. Bit of hide and seek round the border – Crossmaglen, places like that – but elsewhere we – well – agree to lay off each other. What they do to the RUC or the UDR's their own business. I say, this is bloody unfair!

BIMBO: Special Ops?

AUSTIN: No, no. I have their number. In fact – to be perfectly candid – Special Operations are right under my thumb.

BIMBO: I should hope so.

AUSTIN: It's Pira. Pure and simple.

BIMBO: I sometimes wonder if old Copperbottom doesn't run his own special ops on the side?

AUSTIN: (*Brightening slightly*) You do?

BIMBO: (*Sniffing print-out*) Don't know . . . not sure. Just a hunch. We've no tack, no info. Not yet. India . . . bite to . . . should we?

INDIA: (*Weary*) Yes, master. (*Exit.*)

AUSTIN: The bloody RUC! – dropping mortar rounds into British Army Headquarters! There's nothing some of those fellows won't stoop to just to keep us in this damned hole! Call themselves British!

BIMBO: Now, Austin, stay cool, stay cool. It's just what they want – don't you see? They want you to pitch in. Old Mollynocks and Pisspot'll be delighted to see you chaps back in the ring with Pira. And that (*Wagging finger*) we most certainly do *not* want.

AUSTIN: (*To himself*) It's as good as a treaty! We have an agreement! Why, I met with their entire army council.

BIMBO: Now steady on. I want to . . . I want to – (*Stops.*) Could be this isn't quite the right moment to tell you?

AUSTIN: (*Sharp but anxious*) What d'you mean? Have you something you want to say to me?

BIMBO: At ease, old chap. Your own position is entirely secure – as Truman said to MacArthur. You have my word. Never fear.

AUSTIN: Well, what's the buzz?

BIMBO: No buzz, it's the real thing big. I want your chaps to pitch in next Saturday. And I mean pitch in.

AUSTIN: But that's upside down!

BIMBO: No, it's not. Listen. We did it last year, and the year before – in fact we do much the same thing every July now. Dirty Douglas started it. Mind you, it would help if you'd been here for a bit longer. God! I feel I've been here for bloody centuries! And I do wish you'd been properly briefed.

AUSTIN: I have been extensively briefed – *and* I have made a full and intensive study of our position.

BIMBO: Our position! Hoho. Hardly missionary. Listen, Austin, you chaps and the RUC – I want to see them shoulder to shoulder.

AUSTIN: But that's absurd! – we've been letting them get on with the show for a long time now. That's why they've turned the mortars on us.

BIMBO: (*Hand on shoulder*) Austin, Austin, there isn't a shred of evidence.

AUSTIN: It was your allegation, not mine.

BIMBO: No, no. I merely aired the strayest of whims, the most delicate of hunches.

AUSTIN: In any case, the Chief Con isn't here.

BIMBO: Precisely. Why d'you think I asked you to pop in before he arrived?

AUSTIN: I wish you'd put something on the line.

BIMBO: I will, I will. But cool it, please. As I was saying, you'll be shoulder to shoulder with the native fuzz – officially. Actually – I mean on the ground – you'll be standing behind them. They'll be (*Advancing*) out front. And I want you (*Moving back*) to move downstage, say twenty yards. Take up position and set up a real meatgrinder – then (*Taking pencil*) start running it. (*Sticks pencil in electric sharpener*) The Orange lot'll be marching in . . . in – a small town thataway (*Gestures*) . . .

INDIA: (*From kitchen*) Porteedown.

BIMBO: Of course, usual place. Porteedown. It's got some sort of a railway tunnel in it. You go in at dawn and fence the wretched thing off. I'll ban the parade, *they*'ll march, *we*'ll bop them. We always do.

AUSTIN: And you call that double-distancing?

BIMBO: Listen, what we do is put the coppers in the front line.

43

You lay on a few really pukka second lieutenants with loudhailers (*Cups hands*.) . . . 'C'mon, let's be having you . . . call yourselves men, ho-ho.' That sort of thing. A Radley voice is best, we always find. Make sure it's biffed out over those slow tomtoms they always beat. (*Beats time with model plane on table*.) They'll all be pissed as newts, angry as vipers. Tell the cops to raise their dick-guns (*Lifting plane*) – blam! blam! blam! lots of lovely plastic. (*Bashing plane's nose on table*) Turn on the gas then – the sort that makes them shit when they sneeze. Then drop down and clobber them. Send the snatch squads in but take no prisoners. Break as many skulls as you possibly can.

AUSTIN: (*Quietly excited*) Yes, I remember now – police always take a lot of punishment. Damned good. Sort of *omelette baveuse* – slippy, but delicious.

BIMBO: More of an hors-d'oeuvre actually.

AUSTIN: Oh, how's that?

BIMBO: Well, you see that scenario I've just outlined? –

AUSTIN: Yes?

BIMBO: Well, it's pretty much an historic ritual by now. Result is – there's a lot of manoeuvring, lot of shadow boxing, so very few Orange skulls get broken.

AUSTIN: That *is* a nuisance.

BIMBO: I really believe we need to follow on now.

AUSTIN: You do?

BIMBO: I do. You see, between you and me, Austin, the RUC has a secret plan all its own –

AUSTIN: What!

BIMBO: The coppers, some of them, are going to give way at the last moment – going to let the demonstrators through to your chaps.

AUSTIN: Damn me! – another mortar op!

BIMBO: (*Hand on shoulder*) Seems to me, Austin, there's a way of wrongfooting them –

(*Enter* INDIA *with sandwiches,* BIMBO *takes one.*)

AUSTIN: (*Sceptical*) Is there?

BIMBO: If you could simply park a few lorries somewhere back behind your chaps – hide a few sharpshooters up top. Give them the right instructions –

AUSTIN: (*Gunning*) Open up! *bam! bam!* Yes!

BIMBO: Mind you – aimed shots, Austin, aimed shots. Let it border on the reckless but try not to bring down any of their brats or womenfolk. If your lads could waste – oh, say twenty Orangemen (throw in a couple of policemen if you want) – I'd see them right. We'll simply say they were responding to sniper fire and pay them a bounty. My hunch is that if your lads can't let off a bit of steam pretty damned quick things may get a lot worse – before they get any better, of course. D'you get my drift?

AUSTIN: Yep. I'm on target.

BIMBO: Good–good. (*Stretching*) Wish that damned Chief Constable would hurry up.

(HERBY *passes.*)

AUSTIN: (*Briskly*) I say – that man. You.

(HERBY *freezes.*)

BIMBO: Austin, my dear fellow, he's merely menial.

AUSTIN: Ad-vance.

(HERBY *remains still.*)

Advance and be recognized.

(HERBY *still.*)

BIMBO: Herbert, there's a stout fellow – let's not make a meal of this. The general appears to have something to say to you.

(HERBY *steps slowly over threshold.*)

AUSTIN: Masalkhari askari.

(HERBY *shrugs.*)

Masalkhari askari.

INDIA: What on earth is going on?

BIMBO: (*Delighted*) Shush, my dear.

AUSTIN: Masalkhari . . . mwanadamu? mzee mbaya? mwivi?

HERBY: (*Slow, reluctant*) Masal . . . khari.

AUSTIN: Je! Mita ina miiba.

HERBY: Mimi no nyama, (*Chopping one hand with other*) wewe kisu.

AUSTIN: Wewe mchungwa, mimi no chuppa.

HERBY: (*Pointing*) Wewe ni askari, (*Negative gesture*) lakini

45

wewe si bwana sasa, (*Negative gesture*) lakini wewe ni bwana
sasa.

AUSTIN: Ujinga, ujinga.

HERBY: (*Clicking tongue*) Mzee mbaya. Mwivi.

AUSTIN: Kali sana, Hawkins? Hawkins, kali sana?

HERBY: (*Shrugging*) Hawkins kali sana.

AUSTIN: (*Eager*) Batuni batuni, ah! (*Moving*) Batuni batuni, ah!

HERBY: (*Appealing*) Ah, Jesus – Bimbo.

    (BIMBO *folds arms, smiles, is silent.*)

AUSTIN: (*Freezing*) I thought so. The minute I saw him.

BIMBO: Well, well. You are a very dark horse, Herby.

HERBY: (*Defiant*) None o'your business.

BIMBO: Say you so? Say you so? We shall see about that.

INDIA: This really is disgraceful, Herby. (*Pointing sandwich at
him*) You told me just an hour ago – told me the most
terrible untruths. Here, in this room!

HERBY: Ack, India, don't.

INDIA: (*Mimics*) I wuz never outa the narth. Guns, ack, I don't
touch 'em. Never. That's what you said – to poor innocent
little me. And a lot else besides.

BIMBO: (*Peering at* chaise-longue) Bit of interior decorating, too,
if you ask me.

INDIA: (*Throwing sandwich at him*) Oh, shut up! (*To* HERBY)
You've been to war, haven't you? A nasty little war. For a
nasty sneaky man.

HERBY: I couldni help it.

BIMBO: Come, Herbert, all the time here you've bloody been
stroking your ten bean rows and watering the plants as if
you'd nothing to do with us. A most superior sort of
gardener. Anyone else might be forgiven for thinking you
weren't in my pay.

INDIA: (*To* AUSTIN) He used to look down his nose at us.

HERBY: Ack, India, I niver did.

BIMBO: Yes you did, old fruit.

AUSTIN: (*Suddenly*) Put your hands up!

HERBY: Would you fuck off – I will not. I'm not armed.

BIMBO: I'm not armed! Our little horticultural friend can be
holier than thee or me.

46

(AUSTIN *takes ruler from desk, puts it under his arm.*)

INDIA: Come on, Herby, do like the man says. Put your mits up.

HERBY: I will not.

BIMBO: Put them up, I say.

HERBY: Why should I? I'm not in his bloody army. Not any longer.

BIMBO: (*Imperative*) Herbert.

HERBY: Ack . . . do I have to?

BIMBO: Raise, please, them.

(HERBY *very slowly half-raises hands.*)

AUSTIN: (*Turning left hand up with ruler*) I thought so. Left paw – no thumb.

INDIA: And all this time I never noticed.

AUSTIN: A little accident with a simi one dark night.

INDIA: A simi?

AUSTIN: (*Chopping with hand*) Long knife.

BIMBO: Odd, very odd, he's been lying doggo like this.

INDIA: Bow-wow, there's a good boy!

AUSTIN: (*To* INDIA) Call his file up!

INDIA: (*Tapping keyboard*) Oh–oh . . . bloody thing! It's stuck again.

HERBY: You'll get no help from me.

INDIA: (*Fiercely*) You damn well knew how to work this thing all along. Liar!

AUSTIN: Try switching it off.

INDIA: What d'you mean.

AUSTIN: What I say. Switch it off – at the wall socket.

INDIA: (*Getting up, pushing switch*) There.

AUSTIN: Now switch on.

(*She does so.*)

Try the keyboard.

(*She sits down and presses it.*)

INDIA: Eureka! It works!

AUSTIN: Clears the circuits sometimes.

INDIA: Hold on a mo – what *is* your surname, Herby?

HERBY: Find out yourself.

AUSTIN: Adamson. His surname is Adamson.

BIMBO: Ah, old *mwanadamu*. I see. The mark of Cain. At least it's not Adams.

AUSTIN: 1957 – where was he?

INDIA: (*Squinting at screen*) Doesn't say. Fifty to sixty-one, building trade, Midlands – that's all it says.

BIMBO: (*To* HERBY) Naughty, naughty. You *have* been telling lies.

HERBY: So? Can I put nothing behind me? I was rid of it till this (*Nodding towards* AUSTIN) seen me.

INDIA: Well, you needn't have joined our jolly great army, need you?

HERBY: Needn't? needn't? Jesus, you wouldn't know, India. You wouldn't know what it's like t'have ta leave yur own people – move away, go lookin' fer work, find it . . . lose it, move about the place. In a strange counry, wi' strange ways.

INDIA: D'you think I belong here?

AUSTIN: Yull g'back where yu came from. Y've something t'go to. But for me like – there was nothun. I'll tell ye, there was a big oil shortage – a real big one the time they closed th'canal. Wrecked the buildin' trade it did. And I'd no money – I owed money. I was all for the horses in them days. A fella told me one time, they pay what you owe – you join, he says, they pay. That's what he said. So I did. And they paid sure enough. That's it.

AUSTIN: He was with me in the Highlands – in Kenya, that is. A useful – if not absolutely trustworthy – member of one of my countergangs.

INDIA: You seem to know all about him.

AUSTIN: (*Tapping forehead*) I keep my files up here.

BIMBO: Yes, we'll have to beef things up round here. Memo, India, memo.

HERBY: I was kinda happy but – least till I seen this Gook fella.

AUSTIN: You were oathed just as I was . . . (*Prancing*) batuni, batuni, ah! The blood of a live goat – batuni! The turd of a lion – batuni! Chicken shit, a handful of earth – batuni! You ate them, man. Just like the rest of the lads.

HERBY: Aye, and in the mornin' I'd t'walk yer dog.

BIMBO: His dog! What larks!

HERBY: He'd this big Alsatian, a wild thing. Biggles he called it. Biggles!

AUSTIN: A damned good hound. Tore the throats out of several of those bloody maniacs.

HERBY: Ack, we were all maniacs. Every man jack of us.

AUSTIN: Talk like a white man, would you!

BIMBO: Come to think of it, Herb, you don't look exactly white to me.

INDIA: Lick of the tarbrush somewhere.

BIMBO: Whiff of the oil filter, it seems.

AUSTIN: (*To* BIMBO) You know, it was quite incredible – when we got to Kenya we discovered those Bantu hadn't even invented the wheel.

BIMBO: (*Mock pious*) Well, I for one am very glad we gave them the wheel.

HERBY: Aye, we give them the wheel.

INDIA: The wheel? I always get a terribly sore head when I look at wheels going round.

HERBY: Y'd need more'n a vodka ice-cream if y'd seen what I seen – or what I done. And after, we'd get medals – wee wheels I called them – for what we done.

AUSTIN: It was a good scrap, man. We creamed them – at least we did in my sector.

HERBY: Scrap – my arse! I mind you chopped a whole forest down one time – a forest! Twenty thousand women he got – wi'simis – paid them, paid them t'chop it. A whole lunk day they went at it – choppin' till we found them. We were right on the equator, but above us – above us there was this great snowy mountain. And we'd t'watch all day, like waitin' the rats in the corn. (*Raising arms as though firing rifle*) Picked off seven men, from out the last lina trees we did. Then they cut them t'pieces, the women.

AUSTIN: It was a perfect op. I planned it – *and* made it work.

HERBY: I used t'watch ye – y'loved it. You and yur Biggles. Loved every minute. Specially that last bitta forest before they tried run for it.

BIMBO: No sermons, Herbert. I can't bear them. Think of the wheel, the wonderful wheel, the great wee wheel.

HERBY: Ack. Killers n'uniform, killers in ould mackintoshes –
then we'd t'black ourselves up at night . . .

AUSTIN: (*Sharp*) That's an official secret!

HERBY: I dont' give a shit what it is . . . (*Continuing*) we'd
black ourselves up, wrap their sorta rags round us, then go
out trackin'. Y'd catch sight've them skitterin' through
th'coffee bushes wi'home-made guns. I shot them, aye. Else
they'd a shot me. For they were right cruel, those Mau
Maus. They'd get their own kind, pack earth in their
mouths – then slit their throats. The things they done – ah,
yu shoulda seen what vicious things they done.

BIMBO: Herby, dear, this is rather too much *de nos jours*.
Couldn't you two seasoned campaigners talk about
something else? Sex, for example? I believe squaddies are
frightfully keen on it.

HERBY: Ask your man – he'll tell ye.

AUSTIN: (*Uncomfortable*) Not a subject I . . .

BIMBO: Not a subject he . . .

INDIA: Oh Lord, these little public school boys are all the same.

AUSTIN: Whatever your imputation I resent it. And now (*To
BIMBO*) if you'll excuse me I shall leave this particularly
fruitless meeting. (*Stands up.*)

BIMBO: Steady on, old chap. I don't believe we've quite got, as
it were, to the bottom of all this. Herbert, I fear you've
been less than frank with me –

HERBY: I'm sayin' nothun.

BIMBO: Quite irrelevant, old boy. Austin and I must discuss
your recent behaviour pronto. I think you'd better take a
stroll – cool off, the night is young. I shall want to see you
tomorrow morning.

(HERBY *stands uncertainly, reluctant to leave.* BIMBO *points to
window.*)

OUT!

A few minutes later. AUSTIN *clearly uncomfortable and eager to leave.* BIMBO *thoughtful.* INDIA *reading papers at desk.*

AUSTIN: I know everything about him. Still no sign of that wretched police wallah. I really ought to get back and look at the damage.

BIMBO: Austin, Austin, you might at least share what you know with me.

AUSTIN: Why?

BIMBO: We're both on the same side, aren't we?

AUSTIN: Oh, that!

BIMBO: Yes, that. You see, I've been rather under the impression that Herby was carrying information from – not to – a small back room off the road to New-somewhere-or-other.

INDIA: (*Looking up*) I feel ill.

BIMBO: (*Musing*) A tapped line, a tap root . . . hm.

AUSTIN: More like a field telephone – chap's been having a field day. At our expense, I'd say.

BIMBO: You would? Brawn Street, or somesuch name, is where it's at. The fellow's been spying on us.

INDIA: I feel absolutely betrayed!

BIMBO: Darling, we'll simply have to get used to it. Problem is, how do we turn him?

AUSTIN: Turn him where?

BIMBO: Yes, (*Moving about room flapping arms*) well, that *is* rather a sticky question – deuced awkward, if you ask me. Not sure – to be perfectly frank – quite in what direction I'm pointing just now.

AUSTIN: I do wish you'd make up your mind.

BIMBO: Seems to me we've got to bend him back to our interests again – I've got a lot of very high-grade intelligence out of him in recent weeks. Not all of it planted, I'm sure. Or should I simply sack him?

AUSTIN: I'd put him in a sack first if I were you.

BIMBO: You would? (*Brightening*) Maybe we should shove little India in as well?

INDIA: Oh shut up! You've a nasty nasty mind.

(*Noises, shouts, from a small loudspeaker concealed behind portrait of Queen. More shouts.* AUSTIN *clicks fingers, gestures to* INDIA *and* BIMBO *to take cover near window.* BIMBO *points to portrait,* AUSTIN *removes it, then dims lights on master switch.*)

(*From loudspeaker*:)

HERBY: (*Off*) Would yu clear aff! I'm fed up wi'yez!

HENDERSON: (*Off*) Now just you listen to me.

HERBY: (*Off*) Texel – I'm only talkin' t'Texel.

HENDERSON: (*Off*) But he told me to wait for you. I've been waiting – waiting like a dog under this tree – waiting for hours.

HERBY: (*Off*) I mind what Texel told ye – but I heard ye – aye, I heard ye.

HENDERSON: (*Off*) You heard nothing, man.

HERBY: (*Off*) I marked you the day – 'there's bad uns . . . bad uns, sir Secretary uv State – just waitin' in the wings' – that's 'at you told him.

HENDERSON: (*Off*) I had to keep cover man.

HERBY: (*Off*) Keep cover! Keep cover! I believe ye. Know what you are? – a liar. Yis, a liar.

HENDERSON: (*Off*) I won't be spoken to like that! Bloody ignoramus!

HERBY: (*Off*) Is that right! Is that right! Oh, aye – yoor the ones tell us t'eat grass – won't we all eat grass? – no surrender and eat grass. Jesus, I'll show ye. (*Sounds of scuffle.*) Stuff that in yer geb an' see if y'like it.

(*Coughs and splutters.*)

HENDERSON: (*Off*) You . . . ignorant . . . (*Spit-splutter.*) . . . uneducated . . . (*Spit-splutter.*) . . . ass.

HERBY: (*Off*) Get aff! – just get aff!

(*Loud splash and* HENDERSON *shouting.*)

BIMBO: (*Switching lights up, cheerful, flexing hands*) Herby and the Rain King, I don't doubt. I'm so glad I had the entire demesne wired for sound. A most instructive little spat. (*Goes out on to balcony.*) I say, you men, what's going on down there?

VOICE: (*Off*) Go you back inside. I'm bringing them in.

HENDERSON: (*Off*) Hey, take him, take him. You know who I am.

(INDIA *hands Queen's portrait to* AUSTIN *who replaces it.*)

INDIA: This is getting a bit too like Brighton for comfort. Anyone would think we were still in the Grand Hotel. (*Noise of hard and sploshy footsteps. Enter* HERBY *through right window,* HENDERSON *through middle,* CHIEF CONSTABLE *through left. As he enters the* CHIEF CONSTABLE *leaves his blackthorn outside.* HENDERSON *is dripping wet, his mouth is stained with grass juice, his collar and tie are wrenched untidily. The* CHIEF CONSTABLE, *a thick-set balding man with a slight scar on his forehead and a leather portfolio under his arm, relishes his advantage.*)

CHIEF CONSTABLE: (*To* AUSTIN) Your men – where were they? Perimeter, lawns, lake – nothing. Where are they?

AUSTIN: (*To* BIMBO *in official voice*) If you would care to rephrase that question in a civil manner, I may accept it.

CHIEF CONSTABLE: (*Looking round*) Lucky my men cover the main gate. Otherwise this place would be wide open.

BIMBO: Now now, you two, let's hold on a mo. This (*Examining* HENDERSON), this really is brill . . . or brillo – very wet brillo, it seems. I may say, Herbert, that I felt a distinct desire earlier this evening to push your Mr Henderson into the nearest available pond. He bored me – bored me most grievously. But what, I wonder, have you pair been up to? Ohone Kincora, Kincora, as one of your national bards used to keen?

CHIEF CONSTABLE: He was waiting under a chestnut tree, was Henderson. (*Sits down, takes notebook out of portfolio, glances round room, makes notes. His manner is slightly bored and detached as though he's stumbled into a country-house charade.*)

BIMBO: Jolly, very jolly . . . truly *le roi d'un pays pluvieux.* (*Fiercely, to* HENDERSON) Now you know how I feel. (*Flicking* HENDERSON's *tie*) East of Suez Golf Club I suppose? (*To* INDIA) What d'you make of this specimen?

INDIA: He does seem rather low-rent.

AUSTIN: Bit of a wet basement if you ask me.

53

(CHIEF CONSTABLE *notes this*.)

BIMBO: (*To* HERBY) I rather think the basement is where he wanted you?

HERBY: His kind! – sure they're all the same.

HENDERSON: (*Making a statement*) I am a law-abiding citizen who was going about his lawful business after being entertained in this establishment.

BIMBO: Rather too well entertained, if you ask me. Henderson, you're blotto.

HENDERSON: Secretary of State, I'd just like to say – I was trying to tell you earlier only I never got a proper chance. But it's important – very important. That person there (*Pointing to* HERBY) is dangerous. Yes, dangerous. Now I can tell, Secretary of State – I can tell that I don't have much of your respect – I know that – and I have to face it. But what I say to you is – there's some really bad men – hard hard men – that're only waiting to take over this province. And he's one of them. So you may take your pick.

BIMBO: Some choice!

AUSTIN: (*To* HENDERSON) Tell me, why d'you meet the gardener chap?

HERBY: I'll tell ye –

AUSTIN: (*Loudly*) Quiet! (*Softly*) Private.

HENDERSON: Why did I meet him? To stop him, that's why. Make him see reason.

HERBY: That's a lie!

AUSTIN: }
INDIA: } A lie!
BIMBO: }

CHIEF CONSTABLE: (*Looking up from notebook*) Aye, you're speaking (*Pause, as he looks at* BIMBO) with a forked tongue. Delicate operation that.

HENDERSON: (*More droopy, more abashed*) I've waited . . . waited like a dog. And why? Because we've become – become less than any nation. Now – at this time – we've neither prince – nor prophet – nor leader . . . is it any wonder, I ask you? – is it any wonder I strayed?

54

BIMBO: A most affecting testimony. (*Clapping hands*) Now
Herbert, I'd be most grateful if you and your little friend
would leave us – leave us just for the present moment of
course. Escort him to the main gates – the (*Glancing at*
CHIEF CONSTABLE) exceedingly well-guarded main gates
where his limo is doubtless parked. You've been, Herbert,
rather more devious than I'd guessed, and I shall want a
great deal of frankness from you tomorrow morning. Now,
if you please, these somewhat more distinguished
gentlemen and I have a lot of very important business to
transact – alas, they seem to get on with each other as badly
as you and the Rain King.

ACT FIVE

An hour later. BIMBO *stretched on* chaise-longue, *sleeves rolled up, white handkerchief over his face. Lamps on, almost dark outside, a hot, heavy atmosphere.* CHIEF CONSTABLE *and* AUSTIN *seated at a distance from each other – both are immobile, silent, clearly implacable. The* CHIEF CONSTABLE *looks dogged and uncomfortable.* AUSTIN's *lip is curled.* INDIA *clatters something in the pantry. A stalemate atmosphere where no one moves.*

BIMBO: (*Snorts, wakes a bit, belches, lifts one corner of handkerchief*) Even the bloody teleprinter has nothing to say. (*No reaction, he slumps back for a moment.*) Well, if you chaps won't be civil, neither will I. (*Annoyed slams and clatters from kitchen.*)

INDIA: (*Darting out with teacloth*) I do think it's a bit rich. (*Drops spoons out of teacloth.*) Oh bugger! (*Picks spoons up and goes back into kitchen, then half-emerges.*) After all, it is supposed to be a special occasion. (*Darting out*) Well, isn't it?

BIMBO: My dear, you go more native with every day that passes. All this emotion. Cool it do.

INDIA: Well, I do think they could bury their differences for a minute or two. And as for you – you might at least sit up. (*Exit to pantry.* BIMBO *slowly unfolds himself.* INDIA *enters with birthday cake and candles. She sings fiercely, wanly.*)
Happy birthday, dear Bimbo,
Happy birthday, dear Bimbo,
Happy birthday, dear Bimbo,
Happy birthday to you.
(BIMBO *takes deep breath and blows candles out.*)
Here, (*Handing* BIMBO *knife*) slice it, would you.

BIMBO: It's most awfully sweet of you. And? – drinkies, darling? (*Looking at* CHIEF CONSTABLE *and* AUSTIN) I feel like Lord Curzon among the monkeys.
(INDIA *brings side-plates and exits to pantry.*)

Oh ye *bandar*, abandon me in my drear cantonment!

INDIA: (*From kitchen*) Oh, I almost forgot – here, catch!
(*Throws parcel out,* BIMBO *catches it.*)

BIMBO: (*Opening parcel*) I say, how marvellous! – made in
Taiwan. Mm, I do like that. (*Unfurls Union Jack
sweatshirt.*) What d'you chaps think? (*Flicks it like
bullfighter.*) No comment? None? Well, let 'em eat cake –
make a change from grass.
(*Exit to kitchen as* INDIA *enters. She hands out cake.*)
(*Off.*) Sweetie, you really ought to take a slice out to Herby
– make it a nice big slice.

INDIA: But you sent him away with that Henderson thingie.

BIMBO: (*From kitchen*) He'll have slipped back, never fear.

INDIA: Are you sure?

BIMBO: (*From kitchen, wearily*) Sure I'm sure.

INDIA: (*To* AUSTIN, *while moving to window*) I say, you could
try just a teeny bit. He's bound to feel low. (*Sets plate on
balcony.*) Herby! Bound to – today of all days.

CHIEF CONSTABLE: If that's his only cross.

AUSTIN: Oh, I don't know, he *has* been here rather a long time.

CHIEF CONSTABLE: Not as long as me he hasn't.

AUSTIN: Oh, but you were born here, weren't you? A cross you
have to bear.

INDIA: (*Intervening*) Well, I'm absolutely delighted to see that
you two gentlemen have at last found something to say to
each other.

BIMBO: (*Jumping in from kitchen, in sweatshirt*) HOWZAT!
(*Walks round room waving hands clasped above head.*)
Gotcha! You betcha! (*To* INDIA, *sprightly*) Darling, I'll
fetch the drinkies – you sit down. Do. (*Gets bottle of
champagne.*) One can't have enough of this quite divine
cham*pagne*. Oh, and we must have s'more *champignons*,
my love. I do so love those wicked little buttons. (*Pops cork,
pours five glasses, gives first to* CHIEF CONSTABLE.) Oh how
marvellous!

CHIEF CONSTABLE: No, thank you.

BIMBO: No, thank you! you must be joking! C'mon, bottoms up
my tiddly-pom – it's Bimbo's natal day, and Bimbo has

been on this earth a very long time indeed. Yea, before archelon; before the ferny reign of the ginkgo, Bimbo was here. And now – where is he? Marooned on a muddly little shelf like something out of the *Origin of Faeces*. Obsolete (*Mock sob*), effete . . . re-plete. Here! (*Pushes glass forward.*)

CHIEF CONSTABLE: I said 'no', and I meant 'no'. I won't have it.

BIMBO: Austin, here's your glass. India, yours. (*Exit with glass.*) Herby! drinkies! drinkies! Come on, old chap, no hard feelings. Drinkies! lovely drinkies! (*Enters.*) Now then, Mr Copperbottom-sur – what seems to be your little problem?

CHIEF CONSTABLE: No problem. I don't drink just.

BIMBO: He doesn't drink just! Go and tell that to the European Court! Bloody bloody hell! Thrown at every fence. (*Going into kitchen, bringing out plate of vol-au-vents, handing it to* AUSTIN, *then* INDIA) Well, we all have our cross to bear, as someone once opined, and you no doubt chose this one for its simple nuisance value – its most uncivil and extreme provocation. India, fetch him a mineral water do – Evian or Vichy, I'm sure either one will make him feel equally uncomfortable. Oh, do have one of these (*To* CHIEF CONSTABLE) and do help yourself. Take, eat – and take your time. God knows we've enough of it. A thousand, two thousand . . . the number of days I've been here. (*Going over to window*) Light's a bit samey just now, don't you think? Dull but close. Humid. Don't like that. I love it, though – so love it – after one of those quick thrashy rain showers. There's this great brightness. It blinds one. Huge, constant, marvellous light. I know, I really do know I'm in another country then . . . Cloud-cuckoo-land, miles from home. Always this faint crappy smell, I find. But let us not upon these mysteries dwell. Chief?

(CHIEF CONSTABLE *turns but says nothing.*)

I'm worried – yes, worried. To be perfectly blunt I can only speculate on the health of that little police federation of yours.

CHIEF CONSTABLE: Don't bother.

BIMBO: Oh, but I do, I do. I very much and most intensely do. After all, to lose by a round dozen a vote of confidence looks even to an unpractised eye like the most outstanding ineptitude. Every one of my many pejoratives fails me, I may say.

(HERBY *passes windows, stops, eats cake, drinks.*)

CHIEF CONSTABLE: I was called to do a job, and I mean to finish it. There's no one'll hinder me. (*Takes another vol-au-vent.*) As I was saying before, you'll need to tighten things up round here. (*Gestures at open window.*) We're at war.

BIMBO: Of course you're at *warr*, as you so quaintly term it. Or, of course *we're* at war. But war, as someone in the age of reason remarked, is a province of social life. That's correct, Austin, is it not?

AUSTIN: Eh, yes, up to a point, I suppose.

BIMBO: Up to the hilt, dear boy. (*To* CHIEF CONSTABLE) And when votes of confidence fail whole governments fall. The forests echo to the sound of crashing timber. And you don't – as of now – look exactly vertical to me.

AUSTIN: (*Slightly blocked*) Oh, I don't know, after all, you know what they say? –

BIMBO: (*Weary*) No. Please.

AUSTIN: There are three things in this world that are of absolutely no value to anyone. And d'you know what they are?

CHIEF CONSTABLE: I don't, no.

AUSTIN: (*Leaning forward*) Tits on a bull, balls on a pope, and a vote of no confidence from a police federation.

BIMBO: (*Mocking*) Hoho, oho-ho. I'm sure the rotary club will cheer that one, Austin. Here, (*Hands him large cigar from escritoire*) suck on that, there's a pet.

(AUSTIN *subsides, grinning to himself.* BIMBO *turns to* CHIEF CONSTABLE.)

We shall have to dispense with the general's wit and sheer good taste, I fear. Now – between ourselves – let me briefly illustrate the position as I see it. (*Places hands together like praying statue.*)

Yoyo-yoho. (*Moves hands left, then right.*) You–you – goo–gook. (*Repeats movement.*) Result is what's termed in the trade, friction. (*Moves one hand up.*) Plates slide, (*Moves other hand up*) or (*Stops*) jam. Now the problem, as I see it, is that war – or *warr* – aspires always towards an absolute condition. (*Gets up, moves to lamp.*) Not war for a purpose, but war (*Switches lamp on and moves back to* chaise-longue) as the blind explosion of force, a force quite untrammelled by any considerations of policy. Which is why I have to now and then (*Flicking* AUSTIN *with one hand*) bite chaps like these. It's not that they have ideas – perish the thought! but from time to time they get something into their bloodstream and want to go for broke, go for the biggie, aim for that condition of absolute war to which all force aspires. Ergo – it's over to you. (*Lights cigar.*)

CHIEF CONSTABLE: You took your time saying it.
    (*Teleprinter buzzer.*)

BIMBO: I took my time, (*Going over to teleprinter and tearing off print-out*) but then time, (*Reading print-out*) time is something of which I've got simply oodles. (*Negligently lights* AUSTIN's *cigar, turns to* INDIA.) I say, India?

INDIA: Yes?

BIMBO: Take a look at this, would you? (*Hands print-out over, switches lamp off.*)

INDIA: Good Lord! It's dropped through the bottom!

BIMBO: Thought it might be bad news.

INDIA: But I told you hours ago. *And* you didn't take any notice. It was two to the dollar then.

BIMBO: Oh, was it? I never was much good with figures.

INDIA: It says here that sterling is worth ten cents. Ten cents! To the pound! Incredible!

AUSTIN: Oh well, my loot's safe in the Gulf.

BIMBO: I've a cellar bung full of claret and platinum. Lucky really. (*To* CHIEF CONSTABLE) I fear that clinches it. You're on your absolute ownie own. We're pulling out. Can't afford to keep you any longer, old chap. Nice while it lasted.

CHIEF CONSTABLE: You want me on funeral duty, permanently?

BIMBO: Well, yes – you'd make rather a good mute if it comes to that. (*Leaning forward, puffing cigar*) My dear fellow, you must surely realize that the great British people will wear your being on funeral duty till the day of judgement? – and beyond. Of course you're welcome to remain British as long as you want. Most terribly terribly welcome. But the Taoiseach has sneezed within these very walls . . . and the British people said 'Bless you, that's a relief'.

HERBY: (*Popping in, munching cake*) That's a great sweatshirt y'have on yu, Bimbo. Terrific! (*Raising glass*) Happy returns!

BIMBO: Quiet, Herb, I'm trying to vouchsafe something important to your fellow countryman here.

HERBY: Must be a terrible strain for him, havin' t'listen t'you grinding on hour after hour.

BIMBO: Quiet, dear boy. (*Pause.*) Oh, by the way, did you send our friend Henderson on his dripping way?

HERBY: I did, aye. No bother.

BIMBO: Good–good.

(HERBY *moves away*.)

Now, as I was saying, you really must see that while your chaps and Austin's chaps may argue till kingdom come about your place on the ground *here*! (*Stamps foot*) it is at the end of the day, *our* home ground, the ground back home, the homepatch, the holy of holies, which dictates the tempo and which calls the tune. And this is because policy, so to say, is the womb in which war is nourished, and that womb is the nation, which means that war, war can only be waged – waged at length, d'you see? – with the whole force and might of a nation's power. D'you understand me?

INDIA: (*Of* CHIEF CONSTABLE) He's looking a trifle queasy.

CHIEF CONSTABLE: (*With a puzzled innocence, smiling*) It's strange – strange it is – but I feel a bit dwammy. Aye, a wee taste dwammy.

(*Exit* HERBY.)

INDIA: Austin's tight, of course. You've done terribly well just on mineral water, I must say.

CHIEF CONSTABLE: (*A slow, puzzled admiring smile as he picks up a vol-au-vent*) No, I'd guess these fellas . . . never would've thought it.

INDIA: (*Shocked*) Bimbo, you didn't!

BIMBO: Oh, yes I did.

INDIA: (*Going over to pantry*) But there were two plates. One red, one cream. And you told me to keep the cream one back until everyone had gone. Wanted to gorge on them all by yourself, you said. What did you do?

BIMBO: I simply swapped them round.

INDIA: But why?

BIMBO: Well, when one's a chap in one's house – and that a house thrown up by George III's most spectacularly unsuccessful minister for the colonies – when one has such a chap in such a house and that chap refuses, vetoes, turns down flat – drink, how else, and by what route, is one to lead him to the sacred province of inebriation? (*Shrugs.*) So, I simply swapped them.

INDIA: But you gave Austin some before he even came?

BIMBO: My dear, I thought he might sparkle. But I fear (*Looking at slumped figure*) the poor chap's brain is simply too too tiny. No room for expansion there, I fear.

INDIA: You could at least have told me.

BIMBO: Oh, I wanted these leguminous fragments of the godhead to be proffered with the most complete conviction as to their innocuous and fungal blandness. Otherwise, Chief Copperbottom might have twigged? Mightn't you, old boy.

CHIEF CONSTABLE: Twigged? I've a right nest round me now. Swaying – swaying at the top of the tree. Not vertical, no, not vertical. No.

AUSTIN: (*Waking*) I say, I've never . . . never seen him like this before. What's got into the fellow?

BIMBO: (*Offering plate*) Mushrooms, dumbo. They may not do much for you, but at least I've trained your chaps to spot them. It took a long time, I may say. They're not bright. Now I always send a patrol out, my very own particular brick, 'bout five or six squaddies every morning. Watch them at first light sometimes as they fan out across the lawns – giant anglers with dipped rods, looking for liberty caps. It gives me something to do. They may even enjoy it for all I know.

AUSTIN: (*Sniffing vol-au-vent*) Smells familiar. I remember, we lay up for days – a big rubber plantation, half a mile square, at the edge of the jungle. Yes, Mr Wong, Chopper Gleasby and the Ponce. We never missed a contact. Chewed stuff, bit like *pan*, they kept wrapped in fresh leaves.

BIMBO: Oh shut up, Austin. Your spat in Swahili was bad enough, don't give us a tour of Penang as well.

AUSTIN: I'm getting rather tired –

BIMBO: Write your memoirs and be done with it.

AUSTIN: – tired taking insults from my so-called superiors.

CHIEF CONSTABLE: (*In a wobbly dreaming voice*) Now the general, this general fella – he has . . . he has got something . . . something worth hearing. The Gook – the Gook has had . . . an Experience. Am I right . . . or am I wrong?

AUSTIN: Yes–yes.

CHIEF CONSTABLE: Aye, n'experience. Wi'rubber?

AUSTIN: (*Shrugging*) 'Manner of speaking, yes.

CHIEF CONSTABLE: Aye, wi'rubber. And yis lay . . . yis lay out all night?

AUSTIN: (*Stiffly*) Several nights and several days as a matter of fact.

CHIEF CONSTABLE: With – who were these boys? . . . Mr Wong?

AUSTIN: That is correct.

CHIEF CONSTABLE: Aye, Mr . . . Wong. Chopper Grease?

AUSTIN: Chopper Gleasby.

CHIEF CONSTABLE: Aye, that's what I said . . . the boul Chopper. Chopper Greaseby. And the Ponce, was it?

AUSTIN: (*Wearily*) Correct.

CHIEF CONSTABLE: Powerful. Powerful altogether. Don't often get a story out of you boys, do we? But now . . . (*Moving hands like swimmer slowly*) doesn't everything just go out? Out and beyond, out and beyond. It's like I'm under the watter and it's warm . . . all warm. Aye, it's warm.

BIMBO: (*Bored*) Yes, it is warm. Warm it is indeed. (*Lifts carrier bags.*)

CHIEF CONSTABLE: The last campaign, I mind that. I mind it well. Just a young cub I was. (*Long pause.*) It was thirty

. . . more'n thirty years back. Aye, more'n thirty. But it
was coul'. Starving coul'. Lay out all night we did – top of
a railway 'bankment . . . just outside Kesh, or Lack was it?
From Lack t'Lackey, that's a long haul. Over those hills.
Aye.

BIMBO: (*To* INDIA) We have only ourselves to blame.
(*Fiddles briskly with carrier bags and scissors. Exit* INDIA *to
pantry.*)

CHIEF CONSTABLE: Ah, go on there. Listen. It's nothing.
Nothing happened. We were there all night (*Pause*.) – in
the dike of winter. Me an' a coupla B men . . . watching
this quarry they used leave the buses in. Brittle coul' it was
(*Pause*) . . . no one came. No one. Come seven we'd t'rip
ourselves free . . . we were stuck to the ground but – stiff,
frozen. M'uniform was all hard, like this coul' coul' tube
. . . and me inside the thing, soft flesh, aye – mortal man.
When I got up I nearly fell down . . . I'll never forget the
coul' that night. Never.

BIMBO: (*Moving over with bags*) Yes, sounds awfully exciting –
at least rubbery Austin here got his, as he so quaintly terms
it, contact. But enough is bloody more than enough. Bimbo
has endured your stories for much too long – it's time we
played games. Party games. What Austin's lads call, not
double-distancing, no – double-bagging it is. No (*Raising
hand*) – never fear – I shall not invite you to simulate the
delicious moment in the rose garden. That contact is not to
be. But I warn you both, Bimbo expects the most absolute
obedience (*Places carrier bag with eye and mouth cut-outs over*
AUSTIN's *head, then* CHIEF CONSTABLE's.) Now then, now
then, my clan, my congregation . . . I want a little litany.
After me please.
Good Lord, deliver us.

AUSTIN:
CHIEF CONSTABLE: } Good Lord, deliver us.

BIMBO: We sinners do beseech thee to hear us.

AUSTIN:
CHIEF CONSTABLE: } We sinners do beseech thee to hear us.

BIMBO: (*Raising right hand*) That it may please thee to keep and

64

strengthen in the true worshipping of thee, in righteousness and holiness of life, thy servant Elizabeth, our most gracious Queen and Governor.

AUSTIN:
CHIEF CONSTABLE: } Our most gracious Queen and Governor.

BIMBO: Defend and keep her, so may it please thee, and give her the victory over all her enemies.

AUSTIN:
CHIEF CONSTABLE: } Give her the victory over all her enemies.

BIMBO: That it may please thee to bless and preserve Elizabeth the Queen Mother, Philip Duke of Edinburgh, Charles Duke of Cornwall and Prince of Wales, also his consort Princess Diana, may it please thee to bless and to preserve.

AUSTIN: | Also his consort, Princess Diana, may it
CHIEF CONSTABLE: } please thee to bless and to preserve.

BIMBO: And all the Royal Family.

AUSTIN:
CHIEF CONSTABLE: } And all –

(*Loud knock on door and immediately enter* NORMAN, *bothered-looking, clutching several pieces of paper.*)

BIMBO: (*Furious*) That man! That man! the archie-pelagian-plague of my life. The veritable bloody bane. Advance.

NORMAN: I'm very sorry, Secretary of State, but it's just – you said to come back as soon –

BIMBO: Silence! Stand on your head!

NORMAN: On my what?

BIMBO: On your head, dumbo. It's all it's good for.

NORMAN: I'm not sure I understand –

(*Enter* INDIA.)

INDIA: (*Diplomatic*) Do what he says.

BIMBO: (*Aiming a kick*) At once! pronto!

(NORMAN *quickly does headstand against wall where Queen's portrait hangs.*)

My romper-room – mine!

(*Change falls out of* NORMAN's *pockets.*)

That's right, throw her money away! Chuck the coin of the realm into a bloody bog! May not be worth much but at least her head's on it. (*Paces.*) Yes, yes, that's it – my old

school, there was a chap there who could do just what
you're doing now. But he could do something else as well.
While he was standing on his noddle. Oh yes. And d'you
know what that something else was? D'you know?

NORMAN: (*Meek but uncomfortable*) No.

BIMBO: He could fart – yes, fart – 'Land of Hope and Glory' –
loudly – and with great dignity, I may say. I don't suppose
you can do that?

NORMAN: Of course I can't.

BIMBO: Don't be impertinent. Bloody civil servants! I tell you,
to be able to stand on one's head and fart 'Land of Hope
and Glory' requires many centuries of the most exquisite
breeding. In order to bring civilization – *our* civilization –
to such an absolute pitch of perfection one needs –

INDIA: Bimbo, darling, I do think you're being just a trifle
unfair. The poor chap's confused.

BIMBO: Right, right. Down, boy, down.
(NORMAN *slumps on floor.*)
Here, toss him Austin's bag.
(INDIA *lifts bag*, AUSTIN *asleep, hands bag to* NORMAN.)
Now, ad-vance.
(NORMAN *walks up front with bag on.*)
Right, we shall now have the revised version, pronto.
Here I am.
(*Nothing happens*, BIMBO *snaps fingers.*)
Here I am – repeat after me.

NORMAN: Repee . . . Here I am.

BIMBO: Stuck–stuck in.

NORMAN: Stuck–stuck in.

BIMBO: Hopeless Hillsborough.

NORMAN: Hopeless Hillsborough.

BIMBO: And where is?

NORMAN: And where is?

BIMBO: Hopeless Hillsborough.

NORMAN: Hopeless Hillsborough.

BIMBO: It is in.

NORMAN: It is in.

BIMBO: (*Slow, menacing*) Ugly bloody bloody Ulster.

AUSTIN: Ugly . . . (*Takes off bag.*) I want to be sick.

BIMBO: Use the bag, dear boy, use the bag provided. Don't chunder all over the carpet.

(*Exit* NORMAN *to pantry, sound of coughing, tap running.*)

INDIA: Wouldn't you say?

BIMBO: Quiet, girl. (*Kicking* AUSTIN) Wake up, toodle-oo.

AUSTIN: (*Waking*) I thought I heard – it sounded like singing.

BIMBO: You'll hear more, old fruit. I want a song out of you – anything.

AUSTIN: I can't sing.

BIMBO: Don't provoke me. Sing.

AUSTIN: I simply can't. One can't do everything.

BIMBO: (*Menacing*) Austin, I'm warning you.

INDIA: What about – you know . . . something from the Falklands? That would be super. Oh do, please.

AUSTIN: (*Slightly flattered*) The lads, when we stopped on Ascension I recall, they made up a song.

BIMBO: Sing it.

AUSTIN: Oh, I can only remember a few lines. A very few.

BIMBO: Sing!

AUSTIN: (*Standing up and singing in a ranker's voice*)
We're going to kill the wops with phosphorus.
We'll get them with our GPMGs.
They'd better not try to take cover
'Cos there ain't no fucking trees.

BIMBO: (*Briskly*) Marvellous. Wonderful imaginations our boys have. You may sit down, Austin. Now, my dear, whip that sack off old Copperbottom, would you?

CHIEF CONSTABLE: (*Smiling*) I was happy in there. I was, aye. But now, I don't know. No, I don't. I tell you, this has turned into a right queer evening. I've felt a bit lost at times. I have. I'd like to get up outa my chair, (*Tries to raise himself.*) but I cannie do it. No, I cannie do it.

BIMBO: He'll be frozen to the ground again if I let him get going. Sing, man, sing. I want to hear your copper voice.

CHIEF CONSTABLE: Why sing? Why d'you bid me?

BIMBO: No questions. Do it.

CHIEF CONSTABLE: I'm coul'. Feel very coul'. I'm chilled to the bone.
(*Low flash.*)
INDIA: What was that? Was it lightning?
BIMBO: Sing, man.
CHIEF CONSTABLE: (*With a woozy strange innocent anxiety*) I could sing. I *can* sing. But I don't want to – not for you, not for anyone in this room here.
(*Enter* NORMAN *looking pale. He stands by pantry, looking at* CHIEF CONSTABLE, *listening, worried.*)
That man there (*Pointing vaguely to* NORMAN) . . . maybe. He knows me. I know him. Listen if you want. I don't care. Anyhow (*Rising slowly*) it's like this room there's no one in it.

> There is a green hill far away,
>> Without a city wall,
> Where the dear Lord was crucified
>> Who died to save us all.
>
> We may not know, we cannot tell
>> What pains he had to bear
> But we believe it was for us
>> He hung and suffered there.
>
> He died that we might be forgiven
>> He died to make us good,
> That we might go at last to heaven
>> Saved by his precious Blood.
>
> There was no other good enough
>> To pay the price of sin,
> He only could unlock the gate
>> Of heaven, and let us in.
>
> O dearly dearly has he loved
>> And we must love him too,
> And trust in his redeeming Blood,
>> And try his works to do.

(*Hangs head, slumps, looks lost, leans on chair.*) . . . I cannie see . . . I cannie see. (*To* BIMBO) What've y'done t'me? What? What is it? (*Rubbing hands over his eyes*) Blinded me, that's what. He has me blinded. For I cannie see. I cannie see. Where is this? Where is it? (*Pauses.*) He's taken the light from me. He's thieved it.

(*Low flash,* HERBY *standing at window. He enters.*)

HERBY: Come here t'me.

BIMBO: Leave him, Herby. Serve the fellow right.

HERBY: (*Pointing*) Bimbo . . . *get*. From the House a' Treachery to the streets uv Portiedown . . . we know yur bloody plan.

CHIEF CONSTABLE: Aye . . . no burnt offering, nor sacrifice – no oblation, nor incense . . . no place t'sacrifice before thee, or t'find mercy. (*He steps accidentally on model plane.*) Oh, what've I done? What've I done?

HERBY: (*Taking his arm*) It's no matter. Just leave them be. We'll go out now. We'll go.

(*Sings.*)

And I'll watch you right
Through the star-cut night
Beyond the orange tree.

C'mon, we need never go back. Not into that place. Never. *Tiocfhaidh ar la* (*Raises fist*) . . . our day will come. It will for sure.

(*They reach the window, black-out.*)